EVIDENCE
and
MEANING

International Library of Philosophy
and Scientific Method

EVIDENCE
and
MEANING

Studies in Analytic Philosophy

by

ROBERT J. FOGELIN

LONDON
ROUTLEDGE & KEGAN PAUL
NEW YORK : HUMANITIES PRESS

*First published 1967
by Routledge & Kegan Paul Ltd.
Broadway House, 68–74 Carter Lane
London, E.C.4*

*Printed in Great Britain
by Richard Clay (The Chaucer Press), Ltd.
Bungay, Suffolk*

For

E.J.L.

CONTENTS

Contents

Contents

PART TWO

PREFACE

AT various stages I circulated portions of this work to colleagues for their praise and comments. While they were not niggardly in the former respect, they were absolutely unstinting in raising difficulties, with the net result that the manuscript took about three years longer to complete than I had anticipated. For this invaluable help that saved me from any number of serious mistakes I wish to thank most especially W. T. Jones, Morton O. Beckner, E. John Lemmon, and Douglas Greenlee.

The latter portion of this work concerning evaluative discourse has as its ancestor a doctoral dissertation written under Brand Blanshard and Alan Ross Anderson at Yale University. From Brand Blanshard I gained an appreciation of the positions I wished to reject, while Alan Ross Anderson helped me to formulate my criticisms in a clear and forceful manner. It is hard to imagine a more favourable conjunction of advisers.

I owe a special debt to Pomona College on two counts: for the support of a Trustee Fellowship during the summer of 1963, and, more importantly, for its patience with my notable lack of publication while I pursued this project.

Finally, I wish to thank Bernard Williams for the meticulous care with which he examined the text. His comments not only corrected many errors of detail but also forced fundamental revisions in some of the main theses of this work.

ROBERT J. FOGELIN

Pomona College

xi

Part One

INTRODUCTION

IN this work I shall examine a class of statements that I call *warrant statements*: statements that indicate something about the evidential backing for some further statement, action, or choice. It is the dual thesis of this work that natural languages abound with such statements and that a misunderstanding of their character by philosophers (and others) is the source of widespread confusion.

I have used the sub-title *Studies in Analytic Philosophy* in order to give the reader a rough idea of the methodology that I shall employ; the idea is rough since the title *analytic philosophy* covers a wide range of activities that bear at best a family resemblance to one another. On one approach an attempt is made to translate statements of the natural language into some preferred vocabulary, e.g. the statements of arithmetic are translated into the language of *Principia Mathematica* or mentalistic statements are translated into a purely behaviouristic language. This procedure, which I shall call reductionism, usually involves the austere rigor of the exact sciences; the techniques of symbolic logic are often used, and generally, the goal is to establish an exact synonymy between the *analysandum* and *analysans*. I shall not borrow trouble by offering technical criticisms of this technical enterprise; instead, I shall simply say that I do not propose to carry on philosophical analysis in this way.

Another approach to analysis is associated with the later Wittgenstein and a varied group of British and American philosophers. These philosophers are sometimes collected under the heading of ordinary language analysts, a heading, by the way, that is more misleading than helpful. While these philosophers differ widely in the techniques they employ (and even more widely in the doctrines they espouse), for the most part they share the following traits. In the first place they are rarely interested in establishing a reductionist thesis and thus they avoid the formal paraphernalia of reductionism. Most of them, I think, would not only argue that reductionism is difficult to carry out in detail but also mistaken in principle. Secondly, these philosophers tend to think that the main task of analysis is to resolve perplexities that are grounded in linguistic confusions. Finally, they seem to agree that an examination of the actual use of an expression in common parlance can be of some help in resolving perplexities that arise when the expression is employed in a philosophical context.

Wittgenstein is the leading figure in this movement, and while I shall not attempt a detailed exigesis of his difficult writing, I think a few remarks about his way of doing analysis will help to explain the procedures I shall use. A common mistake, and a mistake that obscures the whole point of his endeavours, is to suppose that Wittgenstein takes ordinary language as legislative for philosophical discourse, and thus considers any departure from ordinary discourse, as such, a mistake. This cannot possibly be his meaning, for on any number of occasions he tells us that we can speak as we please, introduce whatever conventions we like, provided only that we keep clearly in mind *what* we are doing and that *we* are doing it.

One of Wittgenstein's theses is that the philosopher often introduces new conventions for the use of ordinary expressions without realizing that he is doing so, and furthermore, without at the same time relinquishing the old conventions. When the old and new conventions are incompatible—as they sometimes are— this produces a particular sort of perplexity, a perplexity that is distinctively philosophical. This interference between the old conventions and the new convention is analogous to the interference between a mother tongue and a newly acquired language. Like the foreigner, the philosopher speaks with an accent, an accent that Wittgenstein could detect, and in his writings he tried to teach others to detect it as well.

Another feature of Wittgenstein's approach concerns the therapeutic character of his method. This medical analogy is often misunderstood, and the misunderstanding forms the basis of a common criticism. Wittgenstein is not interested in removing philosophical anxieties as such; he is not like the psychiatrist who would administer a drug that would cure a mental disorder even if the mechanism of the cure were totally obscure. He attempts to resolve a philosophical perplexity by showing us, or better, by exhibiting to us, the mistake that is the ground of our perplexity. When the therapy is successful, we are not only freed from a perplexity, we also understand why we were perplexed in the first place.

A pattern of analysis is complete, then, only if it resolves a philosophical perplexity through exhibiting the grounds that gave rise to the confusion. The claim that a traditional problem of philosophy is a pseudo-problem is, on the face of it, suspect; the mere fact that intelligent persons have taken the problem seriously gives *prima facie* reason to suppose that the problem is genuine. Thus if the analyst does nothing more than find a way of restating the issue so that the problematic character disappears, this can be taken as grounds for saying that the issue has been side-stepped, not solved. The goal of philosophical analysis is to exhibit the grounds of philosophical confusions and not to find ways of depleting the language so that the confusion can no longer arise.

The reader who has glanced at the contents of this work may find this declared preference for informal modes of analysis a bit surprising. The scattering of symbolic notation and the occurrence of paired sentences (one in plain language, the other in a contrived and artificial phraseology) suggests that I am doing analysis along reductionist lines. But to repeat, I am not interested in establishing a reductionist thesis. I use schemata (what other philosophers sometimes call models) in order to exhibit certain logical characteristics that have been the source of confusion. No grave issues depend upon the exact wording of these schemata, and thus I shall have no qualms about altering phrasing to cope with changing problems.

A persistent problem throughout this work concerns the amount of detail to be included within a proposed pattern of analysis (a phrase that I shall use interchangeably with 'schema'). The more details that can be successfully included within the suggested schema, the more convincing it will appear; but attempting to cope with details greatly increases the chances of error, and even an incidental error tends to cast doubt upon an entire enterprise. I have not found any systematic way of coping with this problem. When I have felt confident, I have developed analytic schemata in sufficient detail to account for subtle differences between closely related sentences in the natural language. At other times, I have frankly admitted that the analytic schemata cannot account for some striking distinctions in the natural language. When I have been forced to take the second course, I have offered the excuse that my primary intention is to show that certain statements are warrant statements, and this can often be done without at the same time exhibiting distinctions between closely related warrant statements.

Thus this work is exploratory and programmatic. In no single case have I carried through a pattern of warrant statement analysis to anything like completion. In each case I have stopped when the main lines of procedure have been laid down and what I take to be a reasonable presumption has been created in its favour. I most certainly have not presented a detailed documentation of the claim that philosophers have generally misunderstood the character of warrant statements and thus been led into confusions. Except in Part Two, where I do examine texts concerned with the status of value judgments, I have contented myself with presenting ideal case studies of philosophical confusion, relying upon the reader to associate the confusion with the writings of specific philosophers. In many cases I think it will be all too obvious who it is that has made the mistake in question, but claims about how philosophers have argued are, after all, empirical claims, and since I have chosen not to weigh down the text with historical documentation, I have also largely avoided making historical claims.

The reader may find some of the specimen arguments here graced with the title 'ideal case studies of philosophical confusion' little more than straw men who are beheaded in a series of empty victories. *Who*, it will be asked, has ever argued in *that* fashion? And the answer sometimes will be, no one—or at least no one of importance. Then why make a fuss about these arguments? To this I have two replies; the first, I suppose, is tendentious, but perhaps the second is a little less so.

The first reply involves the assumption (or prejudice) that the argumentative structure of most philosophical systems, like the narrative element of most poems, is relatively simple. To put this in a way that is only initially paradoxical, philosophical systems

6

are complex just because the philosopher tries to comprehend a wide range of material within a relatively few patterns of thought. Complexity arises, not in laying down the main lines of a position but in protecting the basic structure from the myriad of detailed criticisms. To oversimplify, it is not 'the bit where he says it' but 'the bit where he takes it back' that introduces complications. Now on this basis it should be possible to characterize (and not merely caricature) an important aspect of a philosophical position by means of a pattern of reasoning that has never been maintained in so simple a form. I think that many of the arguments presented in this work have, in this way, a counterpart in the philosophical tradition, but with the exception of Chapter VI, where I examine literature concerning evaluative discourse, I have not tried to document this claim. This documentation I accept as an outstanding debt.

The second justification for examining these arguments should be less controversial. Philosophers have often become exercised over questions that the non-philosopher (or the philosopher of some other persuasion) will consider trivial. 'How many angels can dance on the head of a pin?' This question has been subject to tiresome ridicule because it doesn't seem to matter how it is answered; the relationship between angels and pinheads is of no importance, not even to angels. Of course, those who discussed this question had more in mind (they were concerned about the principle of individuation for non-corporeal substances) and talked about angels and pinheads only by way of an apt example. 'Are there minds other than my own?' This question seems trivial in rather a different way; it does make a difference how it is answered—a great deal of difference—but the answer seems obvious. Certainly there are other minds; Alfred Tarski has a mind and I'm not Alfred Tarski. When a philosopher considers a question of this kind (one where the answer seems obvious) it is usually because there is some special difficulty in exhibiting the basis for what we take to be obvious. There are, then, at least two reasons for examining trivial problems. (1) They can serve as apt examples in the consideration of a serious philosophical issue, and (2) under analysis they can lead us to a serious philosophical issue. I would not admit that all of the problems examined in this work are trivial; going back to the first remark, I think that some of these patterns of argument, though simple, characterize the

7

argumentative structure of historically important philosophical positions. But for some this excuse would be too pretentious, and for them I invoke the reasons enumerated in this paragraph.

From the very outset I would like to acknowledge my indebtedness to J. L. Austin, whose classic 'Other Minds' is the ancestor of this work. Stephen Toulmin and J. O. Urmson have exploited some of Austin's insights, and I, in turn, have relied heavily on their writings. For rather different reasons, that will emerge in the text, I am also indebted to R. M. Hare and P. H. Nowell-Smith. Throughout I have assumed that the reader is familiar with recent British philosophy, and on this ground I have omitted most of the more obvious scholarly references. Furthermore, I have offered detailed criticism of the works of others only when this helps in explaining a difficult doctrine. In this way, I have preserved the one sure merit of this work, its brevity.

I

WARRANT STATEMENTS

I. THE IDEA OF A WARRANT STATEMENT

A WARRANT statement is any statement that indicates something about the evidential backing available for some further statement.[1] As an example, the following remark wears its warranting character on its grammatical sleeve:

> There is strong evidence available on behalf of the claim: 'There is life on Mars.'

Schematically, this expression has the form 'ϕ "p"', where 'ϕ' is an expression referring to evidential backing, and 'p' names the assertion whose evidential backing is being assessed.

Now every warrant statement will have these two components, an expression that indicates something about evidential backing and an expression that refers to the proposition whose evidential backing is being assessed, but these two components are rarely marked off in the grammatically perspicuous fashion of the example given above. To begin with, we rarely refer to a statement by explicitly quoting the sentence that formulates it. Instead, we usually employ a dependent clause, for example:

> There is strong evidence available *that* there is life on Mars.

---

[1] In Part Two this definition will be liberalized so that we can consider the evidential backing for things other than statements.

9

Furthermore, in everyday discourse we normally avoid such formal locutions as 'strong evidence available that'. The following remark comes closer to the vernacular:

There almost certainly is life on Mars.

The reader might balk at accepting the last sentence as an exact translation of the statement that we began with; it is, however, close enough in meaning, for all I wish to say is that it is a warrant statement that indicates about the same degree of evidential backing as the explicit warrant statement that we began with. But the reader may even balk at this modest claim, for the sentence, 'There almost certainly is life on Mars,' makes no explicit reference to evidential backing nor does it seem to be about an assertion (it seems to be about life on Mars). There is certainly some close relationship between this last statement and the explicit warrant statement that we began with, but it would seem presumptuous to invoke this unspecified relationship as the basis of the claim that this last statement is a warrant statement (albeit an *implicit* warrant statement). This, in a nutshell, presents the methodological problem of this work; on what grounds can we declare that a statement that does not have the grammatical form of a warrant statement is a warrant statement none the less?

But before stating how I propose to deal with this methodological problem, let me add one further complication. The paradigm warrant statement that we began with indicated something about evidential backing but did little else. Most warrant statements, however, not only indicate something about evidential backing but also carry additional information as well. Consider the following assertion as a case in point:

Scientists realize that life on Mars is very likely.

I would say that this remark indicates something about evidential backing, but it also gives us a piece of news about the beliefs of the scientific community. Notice that the sentence doesn't *merely* give us news about the beliefs of scientists, for the word 'realize' indicates that the beliefs involved are true. The methodological problem now takes the following form: how can we show that a given statement has the logical character of a warrant statement when its grammatical form does not exhibit its warranting quality, and when the warranting quality is submerged in the additional content of the sentence?

I have no way of dealing with this problem with rigor. In the philosophically interesting, and hence controversial, cases, I shall only attempt to establish a *reasonable presumption* in favour of the claim that certain statements can be profitably viewed as warrant statements. I shall employ two devices in trying to establish this reasonable presumption: first, I shall try to show that the statements under consideration share logical properties with other statements that surely are warrant statements. Secondly, I shall try to show that the assumption that these statements are warrant statements allows us to deal with certain perennial philosophical perplexities in an effective—though not always conclusive—manner. Let me say just a bit more about each of these procedures.

In the next section I shall present a class of statements that I have called *pure warrant statements*. These pure warrant statements will be *grammatically perspicuous* and *logically simple*. They are grammatically perspicuous in the sense that their grammatical form plainly exhibits their character as warrant statements. They are logically simple because severe restrictions have been placed upon the forms they can take. Having presented these pure warrant statements I shall then examine some of their properties in order to gain some insight into their logical personality. Then in each succeeding chapter I shall argue that a class of statements can be viewed as warrant statements since they possess properties that are *strikingly* similar to the properties of pure warrant statements. This, then, will be the first step in developing a reasonable presumption on behalf of the claim that a family of statements can be viewed as warrant statements.

The second step is philosophically more interesting: I propose to examine certain philosophical problems under the assumption that key statements involved in their formulations have the status of warrant statements. At times I shall argue that the philosophic problem is purely and simply grounded on a misunderstanding of the logical character of these warrant statements; in such cases the philosophical problem should wither away. At other times I shall make the more modest claim that a recognition of the warrant character of statements will give us a better insight into the logical character of a philosophical problem. In short, the ultimate test of warrant statement analysis will be its use as a tool for philosophical inquiry.

2. PURE WARRANT STATEMENTS

In order to construct the class of pure warrant statements, let us return to the example of a warrant statement given in § 1:

> There is strong evidence available on behalf of the claim: 'There is life on Mars.'

Schematically, we have represented this statement as 'ϕ "p" '. The first criterion for a pure warrant statement is that it be an *explicit* substitution instance of this grammatical schema. This amounts to the demand that a pure warrant statement be grammatically perspicuous.

Next we shall divide the schema into two component parts and introduce the following labels:

$$(\phi) \qquad\qquad ('p')$$

warrant component   material component

Each label has a certain appropriateness: the expression 'ϕ' introduces the distinctive warranting quality, for it is this expression that makes reference to evidential backing. The material component, in a rather obvious way, presents the *subject matter* of the warrant statement. Pure warrant statements are now further defined by placing restrictions upon the material component and the warrant component respectively.

The easiest way to avoid complexities in the material component is to ignore its specific content by representing it by a propositional variable. For reasons that will emerge in the next section, it is important to distinguish between an affirmative and a negative material component, and we can do this easily enough by using the negation sign 'N'. Thus the material component of a pure warrant statement will come in just two forms:

> 'p' an affirmative material component
> 'Np' a negative material component

Since pure warrant statements contain a propositional variable in the material component, they are not, strictly speaking, statements at all: they are propositional functions. But since nothing crucial will here turn upon the distinction between a proposition and a propositional function, I shall continue to speak of pure warrant *statements* rather than pure warrant *propositional functions*. So much, then, for the simplification of the material component.

Just as the material component could admit of endless variation, so too there are any number of ways in which 'ϕ' can be filled in, for any expression that indicates something about the status of evidential grounds is appropriate. To avoid the complexities involved in this endless variability, we shall limit the warrant component of a pure warrant statement to just two forms:

> Is warranted
> Is not warranted

These two warrant components have the two following abbreviations: 'W' and 'NW'.

To assert that a statement *is warranted* is to indicate that *sufficient evidence is available to establish its truth*. This strong interpretation of the term 'warranted' is reflected in the truth of the following formula:

> If 'p' is warranted, then p.

The term 'warranted' may not have this strength in its ordinary usage; if it doesn't, it will still be *given* this strength in this work.

To summarize, there are four possible forms that a pure warrant statement can take:

> 'p' is warranted
> 'Np' is warranted
> 'Np' is not warranted
> 'p' is not warranted

Or to put this in an abreviated form:

> Wp
> WNp
> $NWNp$
> Nwp

I have deleted the quotation marks because they are cumbersome; the reader is asked to assume their presence.

3. PURE WARRANT STATEMENTS AND CATEGORICAL STATEMENTS

Having defined the class of pure warrant statements I shall begin the examination of their logical character by noting some interesting similarities between statements of this form and statements of the following forms:

> Everything is ϕ.
> Nothing is ϕ.
> Something is ϕ.
> Something is not ϕ.

Using the familiar equivalence from symbolic logic:

$$(\exists x)\phi x \equiv N(x)N\phi x$$

we can translate all of these statements through the use of the universal quantifier and in doing so the following parallelism emerges:

	Quantified statements	Pure warrant statements
A	$(x)\phi x$	Wp
E	$(x)N\phi x$	WNp
I	$N(x)N\phi x$	$NWNp$
O	$N(x)\phi x$	NWp

Notice that the negation sign has precisely the same distribution about the universal quantifier as it has about the letter 'W'. With a slight alteration in traditional terminology I have taken over the A–E–I–O labels and applied them to warrant statements in the light of this parallelism.[1]

Pursuing this parallelism yet a step farther, let us examine the traditional cross classification of categorical statements:

	Affirmative	Negative
Universal	A: $(x)\phi x$	E: $(x)N\phi x$
Particular	I: $N(x)N\phi x$	O: $N(x)\phi x$

---

[1] In traditional logic the A-proposition is not any universal affirmative proposition, but only universal affirmative propositions of the form: 'All A are B.' Similar remarks hold for the E, I, and O propositions. I am thus using the A–E–I–O terminology in a somewhat wider sense than it is traditionally used.

A Square of Opposition for Pure Warrant Statements

We can take over the notions of *affirmative* and *negative* propositions and say that the A and I warrant statements are affirmative and the E and O warrant statements are negative. But the notions of universal and particular propositions have no obvious application to warrant statements. Instead, we shall say that the A and E warrant statements are *strong*, while the I and O warrant statements are *weak*. These conventions are summarized in the following table:

	Affirmative	Negative
Strong	A: Wp	E: WNp
Weak	I: $NWNp$	O: NWp

So much, then, for the development of a nomenclature for talking about pure warrant statements.

4. A SQUARE OF OPPOSITION FOR PURE WARRANT STATEMENTS

From traditional logic we know that the following square of opposition holds for quantified statements.[1]

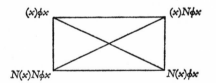

This square of opposition holds for both the Aristotelean and Boolean interpretations of the universal quantifier, provided only that we assume that the universe has at least one member. A similar square of opposition holds for pure warrant statements.

This square of opposition for pure warrant statements takes the following form:

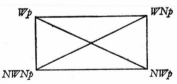

[1] Throughout this discussion I shall assume that the reader is familiar with the standard square of opposition.

If this square of opposition holds, the parallelism between categorical statements and warrant statements noted in § 3 is still maintained. To prove that these four pure warrant statements constitute a square of opposition it is sufficient to show that: (*a*) contradictories hold, and (*b*) contraries hold.

(*a*) Contradictories: '*NWp*' is the explicit denial of '*Wp*' and '*NWNp*' is the explicit denial of '*WNp*'. Hence we can see by simple inspection that contradictories hold.

(*b*) Contraries: To show that '*Wp*' and '*WNp*' are contraries we must establish that they are so related that: (1) they cannot both be true, but (2) they can both be false. That they cannot both be true follows from the principle:

If *Wp*, then *p*.

For if both '*Wp*' and '*WNp*' were true, then both '*p*' and '*Np*' would be true, which is of course impossible. That they can both be false follows from the meaning of the phrase 'is warranted' (p. 13). It is entirely possible that there is not adequate evidence *available* on behalf of '*p*' nor adequate evidence *available* on behalf of '*Np*'. We may then conclude that '*Wp*' and '*WNp*' are true contraries.

We have thus established that these statements form a square of opposition.

We shall now take this logical property of forming a square of opposition as one *mark* of a system of warrant statements. I call it a mark because the formation of a square of opposition is neither a sufficient nor a necessary condition for calling a system of statements a system of warrant statements. Certain quantified and relational statements form squares of opposition, but on this account we shall not call them warrant statements. Furthermore, some families of warrant statements will not form a square of opposition *except under special conditions*.

The italicized portion of the last sentence demands explanation. We derive pure warrant statements by deleting extraneous information altogether and by placing severe restrictions upon both the material component and the warrant component of the remaining warrant statement. With these restrictions in force, the resultant family of statements forms a square of opposition. But it should be quite obvious that a square of opposition need not arise for more complex families of warrant statements. None the less, every warrant statement will have both a warrant component and a material component, and thus allow for four relationships between them: *Wp*, *WNp*, *NWNp*, and *NWp*. This distribution, which forms the foundation for a square of opposition, can be submerged beneath other logical relationships, but in many cases we can bring out the square of opposition by holding these other logical relationships constant.

5. THE WARRANT STATEMENT AND ITS MATERIAL COMPONENT

The formula, 'If *Wp*, then *p*', expresses a logical relationship between a pure warrant statement and its material component. We can express this relationship by saying that a *strong* pure warrant statement implies its material component. If we transpose this formula into 'If *Np*, then *NWp*', we arrive at the further notion that a *weak* pure warrant statement is implied by the denial of its material component.

We can exhibit these relationships between a pure warrant statement and its material component by a slightly more elaborate square of opposition:

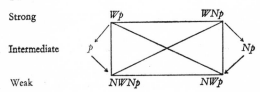

Here the material component occupies the role of an intermediate proposition between the *A and I* and *E and O* propositions respectively.

This logical fact gives us another *mark* of a system of warrant statements. If a system of statements forms a square of opposition (perhaps under special limitations), we then try to find intermediate propositions that stand between the strong and weak propositions. If we can find such intermediate propositions, we then ask the following question: Does it make sense to view these intermediate propositions as the material components of warrant statements? This test is hardly rigorous, but I hope to show in later chapters that once this question is asked explicitly, an affirmative answer can often be given with few qualms.

6. THE RULE OF STRENGTH

In the last two sections I have examined some of the logical properties of pure warrant statements in order to point out marks that more complex systems of warrant statements are likely to possess. In this section I shall discuss a different kind of property exhibited by statements that form squares of opposition. This property is easily misunderstood, and hence is often the cause of considerable confusion. I can introduce this new subject through the use of a logical howler:

(1) If something is necessary, then it is possible.
(2) If something is possible, then its opposite is possible.
∴ (3) If something is necessary, then its opposite is possible.

Once we see the pattern of this argument we can produce others at will. For example:

(1) If something is good, then it is not bad.
(2) If something is not bad, then it's really not so good.
∴ (3) If something is good, then it's really not so good.

Or:

(1) If you are obliged to do something, then you are permitted to do it.
(2) If you are permitted to do something, then you are permitted not to do it.
∴ (3) If you are obliged to do something, then you are permitted not to do it.

And so on.

Now it is easy enough to avoid these paradoxical conclusions by declaring the second premiss of each argument false. And, of course, each of these second premisses is false if it is interpreted in the fashion necessary to yield a valid argument. But it is more interesting to reflect upon why each of these second premisses *seems* to be true. For example, if you are told that you are *permitted* to sign up with the Forest Ranger before and after camping in the wilderness, you will naturally think that you really don't *have to* sign up, although you may if you wish. Normally the use of a statement giving permission indicates that one is permitted to abstain as well; and if this is the point of the remark, 'If you are permitted to do something, then you are permitted not to do it,' then the remark is true for virtually all contexts.

But this does not constitute a defence of the third argument, for if we replace the second premiss with its explicitly worked out interpretation, we get the following result:

(1) If you are obliged to do something, then you are permitted to do it.

(2) If you are told that you are permitted to do something, this normally indicates that you are permitted not to do it.

∴ (3) If you are obliged to do something, then you are permitted not to do it.

Now both premisses are true, but the argument plainly fails on grounds of invalidity. Thus, under one interpretation the argument is valid but the second premiss is false, and under the other interpretation the premisses are true, but the argument is invalid. Similar analyses hold for the other two arguments.

The above remarks invoke a distinction between what a statement implies (or entails) and what the use of a statement *indicates*. The distinction is obvious enough. The proposition 'The Chinese are not to be trusted' does not imply (or entail) that General Grover believes that the Chinese are not to be trusted. But if General Grover *says*, 'The Chinese are not to be trusted,' his remark indicates that he believes this.[1] The use of an utterance suggests things in this way because speech is a form of rule-governed behaviour and unless some signal is given invoking a waiver, we have a right to suppose that the speaker is respecting these rules. That we have a *right* to suppose that a speaker is respecting these rules illustrates the performative aspect of using language. If a person says something that he does not believe (without invoking an appropriate waiver) his remark is not just

---

[1] P. H. Nowell-Smith discusses these matters under the heading of contextual implications (see his *Ethics*, especially pp. 80–87). Virtually everything that is said in this paragraph is more or less a direct transcription of points that Nowell-Smith has made, and I am thus greatly indebted to him. I have, however, chosen to restrict the technical uses of the terms 'imply' and 'entail' to strictly logical relationships; thus where Nowell-Smith speaks of the use of a statement contextually implying something, I shall say, instead, that the use of a statement *indicates* or *suggests* something. I prefer this terminology because it does not gratuitously suggest that there are two kinds of implication (logical implication and contextual implication) that share some unspecified common genus.

a counter-example to the empirical generalization that people believe what they say; it constitutes a *violation* of the rule: thou shalt not make a straightforward assertion that you do not believe. To sum up, the use of language is under the governance of rules and thus when someone employs a given expression we are entitled to assume that the appropriate rules are being followed. When we can draw inference from the use of a statement that we cannot draw from the statement itself, this usually indicates that our inference is grounded on the assumption that some linguistic rule is in force.

Now earlier we saw that the use of a statement giving permission normally indicates that one is permitted to abstain. Similarly, the claim that something is possible normally indicates that its opposite is possible as well. And finally, the claim that something is not bad normally indicates that the thing in question is not particularly good either. All of these cases are the result of another rule that governs the use of assertions, the *rule of strength*, a rule that I shall now attempt to explain.

The rule of strength can be stated in the form of an imperative: *Make the strongest possible claim that you can legitimately defend!* The reader will have some intuitive sense of what is meant by calling one statement stronger than another. Given propositions 'a' and 'b', the assertion 'a and b' seems stronger (says more, contains more information, etc.) than the assertion 'a or b'.[1] And if we had an appropriate theory of implication we could lay down the following sufficient (though not necessary) condition for calling one proposition stronger than another: a proposition 'a' is stronger than a proposition 'b' if 'a' implies 'b', but 'b' does not imply 'a'. We need something stronger than material implication for this definition, however, for if we do employ material implication we will be faced with the unfortunate result that any arbitrary false statement is stronger than any arbitrary true statement, and, of course, there will be other oddities of the same sort.

But I do not propose to pursue this definition of strength in a general form; instead, since I shall be concerned with systems of warrant statements that form squares of opposition, I shall limit my discussion of the rule of strength to those systems of

---

[1] There are, of course, technical difficulties concerning this suggestion, for if 'a' and 'b' are both L-true, or both L-false, or if they are L-equivalent, this claim fails. But, I am not here trying to explicate the notion of strength, only illustrate it.

propositions that constitute a square of opposition. Take as a first example the square of opposition for categorical propositions under the Aristotelian interpretation of existential commitment.

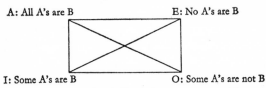

Now by stipulation—a stipulation that squares with our intuitive sense of the matter—we shall say that the A and E propositions are stronger than the I and O propositions. Thus with respect to propositions that form a square of opposition the rule of strength takes this special and perfectly rigorous form: *Do not employ an I or an O proposition in a context where you can legitimately employ an A or an E proposition.* And this special form of the rule of strength has a corollary that will become of central importance later in this section: *Do not affirm one subcontrary if you are willing to deny the other.*

The claim I am making is this: the rule of strength (and from now on we shall be concerned only with its special form) is operative in everyday discourse, and its influence accounts for certain features of everyday discourse. The following example will exhibit its influence on the traditional square of opposition for categorical propositions. Suppose that a soldier is escorting a group of prisoners back from the front line and on his way every last one of them escapes. When he reports to his commanding officer, he states that *some* of his prisoners have escaped. Now in a way, what the soldier says is true; none the less, I think everyone would agree that his report is a bare-faced lie. This lie illustrates a violation of the rule of strength. Here an I proposition is used in a context in which an A proposition is evidentially warranted. Of course, not every violation of the rule of strength will constitute lying—lying presupposes an intention to deceive—but, in general, a violation of the rule of strength will be misleading. There is, however, an important exception to this, and that is the intentional violation of the rule of strength for ironical purposes, for example, calling something *not bad* as a way of indicating that it is very good indeed.[1]

---

[1] Even when the rule is violated for ironical purposes, a signal is usually given to indicate that the statement should not be taken in the standard way. The signal is usually given by the tone of voice.

To return to the example, when the soldier says that some of his prisoners have escaped, he is indicating that he is not in a position to assert the A proposition, 'All of the prisoners have escaped.' Since he is indicating this, and must know that he is indicating this, we consider his report, though true, a patent lie. Or to employ the corollary to the rule of strength, the soldier has violated the rule: do not affirm one subcontrary in a context in which you are justified in denying the other. This corollary to the rule of strength can be viewed as the basis for the fact that in the natural language *subcontraries tend to collapse together*. Since the use of one subcontrary typically suggests that the other subcontrary is true as well, we find ourselves employing a threefold distribution of terms where logically we should expect a fourfold array constituting a square of opposition.

Here are just a few examples of this tendency of subcontraries to collapse, thus converting a square of opposition into a triangular array:

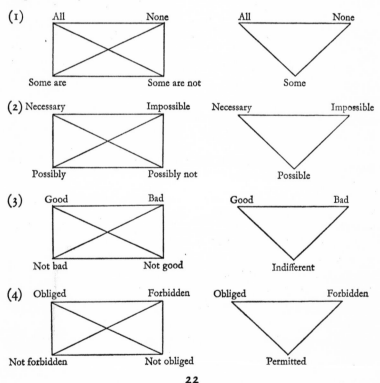

(5)

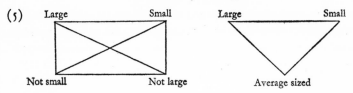

The right-hand triangular arrays do not indicate that there is no distinction between subcontraries in the natural language. Although the use of one subcontrary typically suggests that the other subcontrary is true as well, the I and the O propositions are denials of different propositions and hence can have a different rhetorical force. But even though the distinction between subcontraries is sometimes employed in the natural language, we more often submerge it. Perhaps the best evidence for this is the way such phrases as 'good, bad, or indifferent'; 'all, some, or none'; 'necessary, possible, or impossible'; and 'obliged, permitted, or forbidden' come trippingly from the tongue and have the sound of a complete listing.

The reader can easily convince himself that each of the above fourfold arrays constitutes a genuine square of opposition. He can also convince himself that for each square of opposition it would be misleading to employ one subcontrary in a context where the speaker knows full well that the other subcontrary is false. We can say, then, that the *use* of one subcontrary typically suggests the appropriateness of using the other; and we shall further say that this accounts for the tendency of fourfold logical distributions to emerge as threefold distributions in the natural language.

Once the matter is laid bare, it should be clear that the threefold array does not represent an alternative to the fourfold array for the logical analysis of these concepts: the two patterns are based upon entirely different principles. The fourfold array is grounded in purely logical relationships that obtain between statements, while the threefold array has its basis in a certain rule that governs use of statements, i.e. the rule of strength. But as different as these principles are, it is very easy to confuse them. The three logical howlers that head this section illustrate this confusion in a gross form; in more complex contexts the very same confusion can occur and utterly stymie the progress of philosophical investigation.

Since warrant statements tend to form squares of opposition, we can expect that they will come under the influence of this tendency of subcontraries to collapse in use. To see this in detail we must first examine the potential uses of warrant statements.

7. THE USES OF PURE WARRANT STATEMENTS

Let us return to pure warrant statements and raise the following question: under what circumstances would it be useful to employ a pure warrant statement? Notice that the question makes sense since pure warrant statements are not an invention on my part— they are not part of some artificially constructed ideal language that awaits interpretation. They are a set of statements drawn from common discourse, selected for their relative logical simplicity.

Let us take a specific instance of a pure warrant statement and try to imagine a context in which it would find useful employment:

> There is adequate evidential backing available for the assertion: 'There is life on Mars.'

The first thing to notice about this assertion is that it does not present any evidence on behalf of the claim that there is life on Mars. The statement *does* answer the question: 'Why do you say there is life on Mars?' but does not answer this question in the same way that the following remarks answer it:

(1) Telescopic observation has revealed a variable green area in the equatorial region of Mars.
(2) Spectroscopic analysis of light from Mars indicates that its surface contains those elements normally associated with life (carbon, nitrogen, phosphorous, etc.).
(3) In the equatorial region the mean temperature is sufficiently high to support life. (There are regions on earth with the same mean temperature that support life.)
(4) The atmosphere of Mars contains carbon dioxide and water vapour, the starting materials for photosynthesis.

Such statements *offer* evidence in support of the claim that there is life on Mars, and we shall say that they offer *material reasons* on behalf of this claim. A pure warrant statement does not offer material reasons on behalf of an assertion; instead, it makes a claim about the *status* of the available material reasons.

One thing should be clear, a pure warrant statement cannot do the job of a material reason. If someone demands that I bring forth my evidence on behalf of the assertion that there is life on Mars, it will hardly do to tell him that the evidence is adequate, for presumably this is the very thing he wants demonstrated. But there are occasions where a pure warrant statement will find employment. A strong warrant statement, by indicating that there are adequate material reasons available for some assertion, can be used to *offer assurances* concerning the truth of that assertion. A weak warrant statement, by indicating that the available grounds fall short of adequacy, can be used to *warn* a listener that a statement does not have the status of an established fact.

Let us look for a moment at this process of assurance-giving. On some occasions we fear that our assertions will not be accepted by others. Perhaps our listeners will not grant that we have adequate grounds for the assertion that we are making, or he may not even treat our remarks as serious assertions at all, supposing instead that we are joking, making up a story, pretending, or something of the sort. In many contexts—though certainly not in all contexts—the use of a locution that offers assurances that we are making a serious well-grounded assertion can allay such doubts or misconceptions. Of course, if our listener is deeply suspicious of our assertion, nothing short of producing the material reasons will be sufficient; but discourse normally operates upon a credit system, and on many occasions the declaration of adequate backing will be accepted in lieu of an actual accounting. It is in these contexts where assuring can have some effect that a strong pure warrant statement will be employed; ultimately we shall see (in Chapter V) that all strong warrant statements have as their primary function the giving of assurance.

If we turn now to weak pure warrant statements, we see that their most striking feature is just how weak (i.e. uninformative) they are. If I am told that the evidential backing on behalf of some assertion is not adequate to establish its truth, I am given very little information about the exact strength of the available evidence; it can range from being just short of adequate to being totally non-existent. In everyday discourse, we would rarely employ such an indeterminate remark about evidential backing; instead, we employ such phrases as:

> There is very strong reason to believe that . . .
> There is some, but indecisive, evidence that . . .
> There is little evidence on behalf of . . .
> There is no evidence that supports . . .

Each of these expressions supplies a warrant component for a warrant statement, but for an *im*pure warrant statement; none of these warrant components has been sanctioned for use in pure warrant statements.

But since pure weak warrant statements have so little content, I shall go a bit beyond the scope of this chapter and say just a few things about weak warrant statements in general. All weak warrant statements have this much in common: the warrant statement as a whole does *not* entail its material component. Thus the statement, 'There is very strong reason to believe that there is life on Mars,' does not entail the statement, 'There is life on Mars.' And, needless to say, no such entailment holds for the statement, 'There is no evidence that there is life on Mars.' We shall, then, take this as a defining characteristic of all weak warrant statements: a warrant statement is weak if it does not entail its material component.

What tasks, then, can be performed by weak warrant statements? The answer to this depends upon the strength of the given warrant statement. The remark, 'There is very strong reason to believe that there is life on Mars,' falls just short of being a strong warrant statement in the strength of the grounds it asserts. We might say that this statement offers assurances, but not unqualified assurance—to employ a common expression, this statement offers assurances in a *guarded* fashion. One of the main tasks of *relatively strong* weak warrant statements is to formulate guarded discourse, and, of course, the weaker the warrant statement, the more guarded is the remark it formulates.

If we move now to the opposite end of the spectrum and examine the extremely weak warrant statement, 'There is no evidence that there is life on Mars,' we see at once that it would be silly to say that this statement gives guarded assurance that there is life on Mars. Quite to the contrary, this remark *discounts* the claim that there is life on Mars. I use the word *discounts* in contrast

26

to the term *denies*. To discount an assertion is to indicate that there are not sufficient grounds to accept it, and this is quite a different thing from denying an assertion.[1] The relatively weak warrant statements typically perform this task of discounting. We can then sum up the functions of weak warrant statements in the following way: those that are relatively strong can perform the task of giving guarded assurance; those that are relatively weak can perform the task of discounting. I shall return to these topics in Chapter V, and there argue that the general task of warrant statements is to supply the diction for reasoned discourse.

8. WARRANT STATEMENTS AND THE RULE OF STRENGTH

When the rule of strength is applied to warrant statements it takes the following form: one should not use a warrant statement that is weaker than the evidential backing demands. For example: a group of space voyagers discover that the surface of Mars is very much like Australia, indeed, kangaroos, eucalyptus trees, and duck-billed platypi are to be found there. Under these circumstances, the explorers could correctly report back to Earth that there is life on Mars. Furthermore, since their discovery is surprising, it would probably seem appropriate to offer assurances through the use of a strong warrant statement: 'We have *incontrovertable* evidence that there is life on Mars.' The term 'incontrovertable' gives this statement the force of a strong warrant statement.

But suppose these explorers sent back the following message:

There is some evidence that there is life on Mars.

In the given context, this message is plainly misleading, for this remark which is in the middle ground of agnosticism *suggests* that the question is still up in the air, which it is not. To repeat an important point, this statement does not entail (or imply) that the evidence falls short of adequacy, but the *use* of the weak warrant statement *suggests* this inadequacy since we assume (under the rule

[1] We do, it must be admitted, sometimes reason in the following fashion: Since there is no evidence that there is life on Mars we can be assured that there isn't any life on Mars. The argument makes sense if we add as a suppressed premiss some such remark as this: If there were life on Mars then some evidence for it would have turned up by now.

of strength) that a person will not speak guardedly unless there is a good reason for doing so.

Notice, however, that the use of an intermediate proposition in a context where a strong warrant statement is appropriate is not necessarily misleading. Consider the following A, Intermediate, and I propositions:

> A: There are adequate grounds available for the claim that there is life on Mars.
>
> Int.: There is life on Mars.
>
> I: There are not adequate grounds available for the claim that there is not life on Mars.

By definition neither the A proposition nor the Intermediate proposition is a weak warrant statement, and thus the use of an Intermediate proposition in place of an A proposition cannot be a violation of the rule that one should not use a weak warrant statement when there is no practical necessity to do so.

Let us look more closely at the relationship between an A proposition and the Intermediate proposition. We already know that the Intermediate proposition is the material component of a strong warrant statement, and '$Wp \rightarrow p$' characterizes the logical relationship between them.[1] It should go without saying that the implication does not hold in the opposite direction. We cannot maintain the doctrine '$p \rightarrow Wp$', for presumably there are endlessly many true statements for which there are not adequate grounds *available*. A relationship does run in this direction.

> The *use* of an unguarded statement suggests that no guarding is needed, i.e. it suggests that there are adequate grounds available for what is being asserted.[2]

Thus the use of the intermediate proposition *suggests* the adequacy of grounds that is explicitly stated in a strong warrant statement.

But if the intermediate proposition suggests the adequacy of grounds, again we seem faced with the question: what distinctive role is played by strong warrant statements? We can answer this by reflecting upon the different effects of (1) suggesting the adequacy of grounds, and (2) explicitly declaring this. As indicated

---

[1] Throughout, the arrow will be used as a sign for entailment.

[2] Compare this with the doctrine found in Nowell-Smith's discussion of contextual implication: '*Rule 2*. A speaker contextually implies that he has what he himself believes to be good reasons for his statement' (*Ethics*, p. 81).

earlier, the use of a strong warrant statement underscores the claim for adequate grounds and thus makes it known that we are not speaking in an ill-considered fashion. A strong warrant statement will find employment where giving assurance can serve some useful purpose. In such a context the use of an intermediate proposition is not misleading, although it may be poor strategy, since a failure to give assurances where they are needed may invoke a needless challenge.

9. THE PROGRAMME FOR SUCCEEDING CHAPTERS

In this chapter I have introduced notions that will find extensive use in the remainder of this work; the examination of the logical properties of pure warrant statements and the discussion of the rule of strength are two examples of this. I have also introduced a technical vocabulary which not only provides economic modes of reference but also singles out certain features of warrant statements that are of recurrent interest.

But if successful, this chapter should serve a more important function; it should give the reader an informal sense of the character of warrant statements. In succeeding chapters I shall argue that certain statements are warrant statements, but since these arguments, as I have already indicated in the Introduction, will fall short of proof, I will have to appeal in the end to the reader's sense of what a warrant statement is like. The primary intention of this arid chapter has been to provide such a sense.

II

THE ALETHIC MODALITIES

IN this chapter I shall examine the family of concepts that includes necessity, possibility, and impossibility: the so-called alethic modalities. The point of this chapter is to show that it is profitable to view assertions employing these concepts as warrant statements. But I do not propose to start out by dealing with so complex a notion as necessity; instead, I shall begin by examining the closely related but relatively less complex notion of *certainty*.[1]

In discussing certainty I wish, among other things, to take into account its use in common parlance; and the first thing we notice when we turn to common parlance is that the plain man uses this notion with more freedom than most philosophers would deem appropriate.[2] In particular, the idea that certainty is closely related to the *a priori* is refuted by virtually every occurrence of this notion in everyday discourse. Under warrant statement analysis we shall see that the plain man's seemingly promiscuous use of this concept is quite justified, and that the arbitrary restrictions sometimes insisted upon by philosophers are often philosophic axe-grinding taking the form of linguistic fiat.

---

[1] The reasons for saying that certainty is relatively less complex than necessity will emerge in the chapter.

[2] Norman Malcolm is a notable exception to this claim. See in particular his essay 'The Verification Argument' which has been reprinted in his *Knowledge and Certainty*, Prentice-Hall (Englewood Cliffs, 1963).

2. SOME LOGICAL PROPERTIES OF CERTAINTY STATEMENTS

Statements involving the notion of certainty come in a variety of grammatical forms due to the fact that it can be expressed adjectivally (certain), adverbially (certainly), as well as in the form of a noun (certainty); and I am sure if we were to examine these grammatical forms carefully, we would find that they express subtle—and perhaps philosophically important—differences. But I do not propose to carry the analysis of certainty to this fine a grain, and thus I shall use these grammatical structures as being more or less equivalent in meaning.

There is, however, one grammatical distinction that I would like to take seriously: some statements of certainty include a biographical content, i.e. a reference to who it is that is certain; other statements of certainty lack this biographical content. This difference is illustrated by the two following sets of sentences:

(*a*) I am certain that there is life on Mars.
Jones is certain that there is life on Mars.
Astronomers are certain that there is life on Mars.

(*b*) There is certainly life on Mars.
Life on Mars is a certainty.
It is certain that there is life on Mars.

The first set of sentences have a great deal in common with epistemic statements (i.e. statements involving the verb 'to know'), for epistemic statements usually—though not always—carry such a biographical content. Since I shall discuss epistemic statements in the next chapter, I shall, in this chapter, say little about certainty statements of this first form.[1]

Of the three sentences under (*b*), the third is logically most perspicuous since we can easily break it into two components and then apply the following labels:

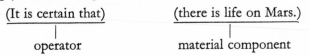

(It is certain that)   (there is life on Mars.)

         operator   material component

We now ask the question: does it make sense to treat the operator in this assertion as the warrant component of a warrant statement?

[1] By this move we also avoid the interesting but difficult notion of *feelings of certainty*. As a matter of fact, I have grave doubts about the existence of a feeling called certitude, but in this work I do not propose to pursue the matter.

Needless to say, I wish to answer this question in the affirmative.

To begin with, the following inferential chain lays the foundation for a close formal similarity between certainty statements and pure warrant statements:

It is certain that there is life on Mars.
↓
There is life on Mars.
↓
It is not certain that there is not life on Mars.

If we abbreviate the operator by the letter '*C*' and the material component by a propositional variable, the chain takes the following schematic form:

A: *Cp*.
↓
Int.: *p*.
↓
I: *NCNp*.

And since the very same inferential chain holds if we replace '*p*' by '*Np*', the following square of opposition emerges for certainty statements with its striking similarity to the square of opposition for pure warrant statements:

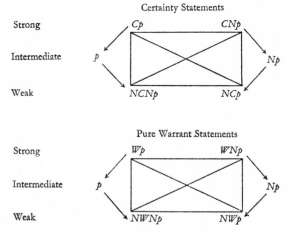

The ground of the square of opposition for certainty statements is, of course, the principle:

$$Cp \to p$$

Thus a defence of this principle will constitute a defence of the whole system of standard relationships. The only objection that I can think of rests upon a transparent confusion. Someone might argue in the following way: 'In the past, people have been certain about all sorts of things that later turned out to be false, hence something can be certain but at the same time false; thus "*Cp*" does not entail "*p*".' But notice that the counter-example concerns *people's* certainty, not the certainty of the *assertion*, and since I have made no claims about this first sort of certainty-statement, the criticism is out of place.

I have avoided statements of the form 'A is certain that *p*' because I am not at all sure about the strength of such remarks. In some contexts it seems decidedly odd to say that a person *is* certain of something, yet that which he is certain of is false; in such contexts we retreat to the weaker remark that he *feels* certain. But in other contexts it seems perfectly all right to say that a person is certain of something that is false. Should I say that Columbus *was* certain or *felt* certain that the earth was pear-shaped? Here, it seems to me, usuage is unclear. Perhaps—and this is a very tentative suggestion—the matter can be handled along the following lines. The biographical content of remarks of the form 'A is certain that *p*' weakens the assertion so that we will accept the inference:

$$\frac{\text{A is certain that } p.}{\therefore \quad p}$$

only on the proviso that we grant A's expertise with respect to *p*. When this proviso is met, such remarks have the force of strong pure warrant statements; when it is not met, they lack this force; expressions like 'feels certain' are used to avoid ambiguity concerning strength.

In passing, we might note that the term '*un*certain' does not appear on the square of opposition. The word 'uncertain' is a reflection of the rule of strength for we use it to indicate that both subcontraries hold at once. Notice that the sentence, 'The existence of life on Mars is an uncertainty,' stands in opposition to *both* of the following sentences:

It is certain that there is life on Mars.
It is certain that there is no life on Mars.

3. THE FUNCTION OF CERTAINTY STATEMENTS

In the previous section we noted a striking parallelism between certainty statements and pure warrant statements, a parallelism that is so striking that the reader may take it as sufficient proof that certainty statements are a kind of warrant statement. A further similarity concerning the *function* of certainty statements will give additional support to this intended conclusion.

In the previous chapter (§ 7) we noted that strong pure warrant statements can be used in giving assurance. Here we may note that strong certainty statements can perform just the same task:

Assuring: It is certain that there is life on Mars.

We also noted that weak pure warrant statements can be used for discounting, but since they are so weak, they could hardly be used for making guarded statements. The same is true for the weak certainty statements we have considered thus far:

Discounting: It is not certain that there is life on Mars.

If, however, we enrich certainty statements so that the operator contains various modifying adjectives, we can also find instances of guarding.

Guarding: It is *virtually* certain that there is life on Mars.

By replacing the word 'virtually' by other modifying phrases or words, we can indicate varying degrees of evidential backing.

It thus seems that there is a close logical isomorphism between certainty statements and pure warrant statements, and a close isomorphism with respect to function as well. Both of these facts create a strong presumption in favour of a warrant statement approach to certainty statements. But an even better way of defending this pattern of analysis is to tentatively accept it and then see where it leads. If it is correct, it should help us to make sense out of further properties of these statements; if it is incorrect, it should lead us into mysteries and muddles. As a first test, let us apply this pattern of analysis to *kinds* of certainty.

4. KINDS OF CERTAINTY

In everyday speech we not only indicate that things are certain, we also often state that they are certain in a particular way. We thus talk about historical certainties, political certainties, economic certainties, mathematical certainties, etc. There seem to be as many kinds of certainty (and uncertainty as well) as there are kinds of reasons that can be brought forth in behalf of a claim.[1]

Under warrant statement analysis we can provide for different kinds of certainty by a simple device. A pure warrant statement takes the following form as an A proposition:

There are adequate grounds available for *p*.

To provide for kinds of certainty, we merely expand the warrant component of pure warrant statements in the following way:

$$\underline{\text{(There are adequate grounds of a } \theta \text{ kind for)}}$$
$$|$$
warrant component

Thus to say that something is certain in a particular way is to assert that it is warranted on a particular sort of grounds. This is hardly much of an advance, but as we shall see later (in § 10), this same schema can be used for the analysis of necessity statements.

5. DEGREES OF CERTAINTY

Unqualified certainty statements stand at the end-points of a continuum that can be represented in the following way:

$$P \text{ is certain } (\dots\dots\dots) \ Np \text{ is certain.}$$
$$|$$
$$P \text{ (or } Np) \text{ is uncertain.}$$

Since certainty claims stand at the end-points of this continuum, it makes only metaphorical sense to talk about *degrees* of certainty. Typically, when we qualify certainty claims we are indicating that the evidential backing falls fairly close to one of the end-points on the evidential continuum. Thus we speak of things being nearly certain, quite certain, virtually certain, etc., and these are standard guarding phrases. We do not, however, speak of things being only slightly certain. In the mid-range of the evidential continuum we employ a different family of terms, namely, those involving the notion of probability.

[1] In saying this, of course, I am not committed to the existence of certainties in any of these fields. I am merely saying that such claims are used and make sense. For the moment, at least, I am only trying to understand them, not to assess them.

To provide for this additional reference to degrees of certainty, we make a further addition to the structure of the warrant component:

$$\underline{\text{(There are } \phi \text{ grounds of a kind } \theta \text{ available for)}}$$
$$|$$
$$\text{warrant component}$$

Here ϕ can be filled in with any adjective that indicates the strength (or completeness) of the available grounds. This pattern not only allows us to deal with degrees of certainty, it also provides a schema for probability statements—a topic that I will now turn to.

6. PROBABILITY STATEMENTS

There is an obvious kinship between probability statements and statements of certainty. For example, the following remarks seem to amount to much the same thing:

> Life on Mars is a virtual certainty.
> Life on Mars is very highly probable.

As far as I know, there is no non-technical locution in the English language that indicates that the probability has the strength of adequacy, or, as a mathematician would say, a value of 1. In common parlance something with the probability of 1 would not be a matter of probability at all.[1] In any case, informal probability statements find their chief employment between the end-points of evidential status. I think we can safely say that informal probability statements simply provide another means for indicating the strength of evidential backing and hence are warrant statements.

7. NUMERICAL PROBABILITY STATEMENTS

In formal writing a numerical probability statement often takes the following form: 'Pr . $(e) = n$', where 'e' is some event and 'n' a numerical value. If we adopt the convention that the values for 'n' are the real numbers from 0 to 1, where a 0 probability indicates that the event certainly will not occur and the value 1

---

[1] I will not insist upon this point since nothing important turns upon it. We do, it must be admitted, assert that things are utterly improbable, and this would seem to have the same force as saying that its denial is certain.

indicates that it certainly will, we at once see the propriety of the following standard axiom of probability theory: if the probability of e occurring is m, then the probability of the non-occurrence of e is 1 minus m. At the limiting cases (1 and 0), this axiom yields the following square of opposition:

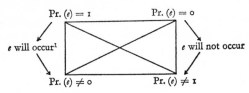

The intermediates hold because assigning a probability of 1 to an event commits us to saying that it will occur, and assigning a probability of 0 to an event commits us to saying that it will not occur. Thus, in the limiting conditions numerical probability statements exhibit the logical properties of pure warrant statements.

Because of this logical parallelism and the obvious kinship between numerical probability statements and certainty statements I shall say that numerical probability statements indicate the strength of available evidence and hence are warrant statements. The use of numerical probabilities normally suggests a rigorous assessment of evidential strength, and this in itself has a certain assurance-giving quality. This is not always the case, however; we sometimes use these statements with the same informality that we use non-numerical probability statements, as, for example, when I say there is a fifty-fifty chance that I can attend a meeting. But usually the use of a numerical probability statement is taken to indicate that the evidential assessment has involved such rigorous techniques as statistical analysis or the application of the probability calculus.

8. PROBABILITY STATEMENTS AND THEIR GROUNDS

A failure to recognize the warrant quality of numerical probability statements usually rests upon a natural confusion: this is the tendency to equate the meaning of a statement with the

---

[1] The tense of the intermediate proposition is determined by the temporal setting, and thus it need not be in the future tense. We can just as well assign probabilities to past and present events.

grounds that are used to support it. With respect to numerical probability statements, this confusion usually takes the form of reducing numerical probability statements to simple statistical statements. I hold this to be a mistake, and a mistake that raises gratuitous puzzles concerning the logical status of probability statements.

I can best exhibit this mistake by means of an example. It is a statistical fact that in casting a single die, a three will come up about one-sixth of the time. From this statistical statement we *may* go on to make the probabilistic judgment: in casting a single die the chances are one in six that it will come up a three. Now compare these two remarks:

(1) In casting a single die, a three will tend to come up one sixth of the time.

(2) In casting a single die, the chances are one in six that *it* will come up a three.

There is a strong temptation to treat the second statement as either (1) synonymous with the first statement, or (2) a specific instance of the first statement. But neither of these interpretations will do, for the first sentence indicates something about a frequency in a sequence of events, while the second statement concerns a single event, and it makes no sense to employ the notion of a frequency with respect to a single event. Hence the second statement is neither synonymous with nor a specific instance of the first statement.

It might be argued that the second statement is elliptical for a rather complex statistical statement, something of the following sort:

A single cast of the die is a member of a sequence of events in which three tends to come up one-sixth of the time.

But even this translation will not do, for there are occasions when we would be unwilling to convert the statistical frequency into a numerical probability. Before we make this move we demand assurances concerning such matters as the fairness of the sample, and this in itself shows an important difference between probability statements and statistical statements.

We can correctly explain the relationship between statistical statements and probability statements in the following way. On many occasions the available evidence is not sufficient to allow us to say that a given event either will or will not occur. We may know, however, that events of this kind tend to occur with a certain frequency under certain conditions, and this information constitutes evidence with respect to the claim that the event will occur. To use the terminology introduced in Chapter I, the statistical statements present *material reasons* in behalf of the *material component* of a probability statement; the probability statement itself offers an assessment of the available material reasons. Thus, a probability statement stands to a statistical statement as a warrant statement stands to the material reasons for its material component.

Stephen Toulmin has made this same point in different and less technical language:

> To attempt to define what is meant by the probability of an event in terms of such things [as (say) frequencies or proportions of alternatives alone] is to confuse the meaning of the term 'probable' with the grounds for regarding the event as probable, i.e., with the grounds for expecting it; and, whatever we do or do not mean by 'probability,' whether or no the word can properly stand on its own, these two things are certainly distinct.[1]

Indeed, a great deal that Toulmin has said can be used in support of warrant statement analysis, and in the next section I shall say a bit more about his treatment of probability.

9. TOULMIN ON PROBABILITY

The reader familiar with Stephen Toulmin's writings on probability will recognize a profound indebtedness that I gladly acknowledge. There are, however, some important differences between our approaches that are worth examining in detail since they draw attention to some of the salient features of a warrant statement pattern of analysis.[2]

Toulmin's treatment of probability statements is explicitly modelled after J. L. Austin's discussion of the verb 'to know' in the essay 'Other Minds'. In this essay, Austin suggests a very close kinship between the verb 'to know' and the verb 'to

[1] *The Uses of Argument*, Cambridge University Press (Cambridge, 1958), p. 68.
[2] This discussion will be based upon the second chapter of Toulmin's *The Uses of Argument*. Here Toulmin combines his earlier criticisms of Kneale and Carnap.

promise'. To use terminology that Austin developed later, the remark 'I promise to do such and such' is a *performative utterance*, a remark that does not describe anything, but rather, makes something the case. When I say 'I promise' (under the appropriate circumstances) I am *assuming* an obligation and not making a report about an obligation. Austin broadly hints that first person present indicative sentences using the very 'to know' have much the same status as promise-making sentences.[1] Toulmin, in a section headed 'I Know, I Promise, Probably',[2] quotes Austin's doctrine with approval and then concludes his discussion with the following remark:

> When I say 'S is probably P', I commit myself guardedly, tentatively, or with reservations to the view that S is P, and (likewise guardedly) lend my authority to that view.[3]

As it stands, I have no objection to this statement; it formulates a true (and important) doctrine about the commitment involved in *using* a probability statement. But Toulmin's comparison between probability statements and promise-making statements suggests that he is making a much stronger claim, in fact, that he is offering us an *analysis* of probability statements. He seems to suggest that the statement 'S is probably P' is pretty much equivalent to the remark:

> I commit myself guardedly (tentatively or with reservation) to the view that S is P, and (likewise guardedly) lend my authority to that view.

Now this remark *is* a performative utterance, for in making it we are not making an assertion (that could be either true or false) about a commitment; we are assuming a commitment. But for this very reason that the utterance can neither be true nor false it must, it seems to me, fail as the proper analysis of 'S is probably P'; for whatever else is true about probability statements, they certainly put forward truth claims.

In sum, then, if Toulmin is offering an analysis of probability statements as performatives, we part company in an important way. But even if we disagree on this point, we are largely in agreement about what probability statements *are not*. They are

---

[1] I shall say more about Austin's discussion of the verb 'to know' in § 3 of the next chapter.

[2] *The Uses of Argument*, pp. 47 ff.   [3] Ibid., p. 53.

not reports about mental states (the subjectivist view), nor are they reports of statistical frequencies (one version of the objectivist view). Furthermore, there is no need to distinguish two senses of the word 'probability' (probability$_1$ and probability$_2$, *a la* Carnap). In fact, on most philosophic issues concerning probability I am in agreement with Toulmin.

10. PROBABILITY EXPRESSIONS IN COMPLEX SETTINGS

When a probability expression occurs within a complex setting, there is often no simple way of converting the total statement into an explicit warrant statement. This can be brought out by examining the following list of statements:

(1) Smith's victory *seemed* highly improbable, but he won none the less.

(2) Smith's victory *was* highly improbable, but he won none the less.

(3) A run of eight consecutive wins is highly improbable, but it sometimes happens none the less.

(4) Smith's run of eight consecutive wins was highly improbable, but it happened none the less.

In (1) a relatively strong warranting expression is placed within the scope of a weak warranting expression—we are not stating what the probability is, but only how it *seemed* at some time in the past—thus there is no logical jolt in passing from the first half of the remark to the second half. (2) has something of the same character, but is a bit more complex. Notice that it is *not* equivalent to the following assertion, where the verb governing the probability claim is changed from the past tense to the present tense:

(2') It is highly improbable that Smith won the election, but he won none the less.

Here we do have a discontinuity between the two halves of the assertion, for in the first part we give strong, though slightly guarded, assent to the denial of a proposition, and then in the next breath we affirm it in an unqualified way. This, it seems to me, *is* decidedly odd, and unless this oddness is being played upon for its special effects, I think that we would be at a loss to know what to make of it. (2) avoids this oddness because it has an *amphibious* character; in the first part of the sentence a probability judgment is made from the *assumed* perspective of the past, while in the second part we are making an unqualified statement from within the present context. The difference between (1) and (2) comes to this: in (1) we *state* how things seemed at some past time, while in (2) we dramatically speak from the past perspective. Thus (1) is not amphibious in the way that (2) is.

Amphibious statements will bear closer scrutiny, for they occur fairly often, and a misunderstanding of them can form the basis of criticisms for virtually everything maintained in this work. To cite another example of an amphibious statement, this time not one that employs warranting expressions, we can imagine an anthropologist speaking in the following way:

> The natives are now asking their rain god Lorba to replenish their wells, illustrating once more the tendency to project through deification persistent cultural needs.

In the first half of this sentence a description is offered from the perspective of the natives engaged in the ritual; in the second half of the sentence a judgment is made from an entirely different perspective, that of the speaker himself. If we ignore the amphibious character of the sentence as a whole, we can derive a claim that neither the natives nor the speaker would accept:

> The natives are now asking their projection to replenish their wells.

In anticipation of later discussion, here are two more examples of warrant statements with an amphibious character:

> I saw white rats scaling the hospital wall, but, of course, there weren't any rats there at all.
>
> I just knew that Harold would come; that's why I was so surprised when he didn't show up.

Sentence (4), like (2), also has an amphibious character, but to bring this out, it will help to look at sentence (3). To say that a string of eight consecutive wins is highly improbable is not to make a claim about a specific event, thus we are not giving our guarded assent to the non-occurrence of a particular happening. Instead, we are stating a general probabilistic principle in virtue of which a specific statement can be made on a suitable occasion. In

(4) we subsume a happening under this principle, but then go on to assert the occurrence of the event, presumably on *other* than these probabilistic grounds. There is no logical conflict here, since the very point of the phrase 'highly probable'—as opposed to 'certain'—is to leave open the possibility of an occasional exception; nor does the sentence involve some weaker kind of incompatibility, for in the second half of the sentence we abandon the limited perspective adopted in the first half. There is no simple way of rendering statements of the form 'ϕ was highly improbable, but it happened none the less' as direct warrant statements, but once we grasp the amphibious character of such a statement, it is easy enough to describe the function of the warranting expression it contains.

II. NECESSITY AND POSSIBILITY

With the discussion of certainty and probability behind us, we are now better equipped to take on the more difficult notions of necessity, possibility, and impossibility, the so-called alethic modalities. We can begin by noting a wide range of properties that these statements share with pure warrant statements and with certainty statements, and in this way start building a case for a warrant statement analysis of necessity statements.

(*a*) Logical Isomorphisms. The alethic modalities constitute a square of opposition complete with intermediate propositions:

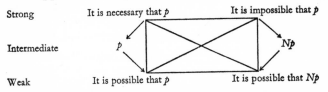

The similarity becomes even more striking if we abbreviate the operator 'it is necessary that' by the symbol '□', and then use this operator to define (by standard modal equivalences) the other three. We can then compare the following fourfold arrays:

	Alethic modalities	Pure warrant statements	Certainty statements
A	$\Box p$	Wp	Cp
E	$\Box Np$	WNp	CNp
I	$N\Box Np$	$NWNp$	$NCNp$
O	$N\Box p$	NWp	NCp

(*b*) Functional Similarities. The alethic modal statements can perform the three standard tasks of warrant statements: assuring, discounting, and guarding.

Assuring: 'Life on Mars is impossible' is assurance-giving with respect to the claim that there is no life on Mars.

Guarding: 'There is a strong possibility that there is life on Mars' is guarded with respect to the claim that there is life on Mars.

Discounting: The last line of the following lyric is discounting with respect to the lines that precede it:

> Oh! Jonah he lived in a whale.
> Oh! Jonah he lived in a whale.
> He made his home in
> That fish's abdomen;
> It ain't necessarily so.

(*c*) Kinds of Necessity and Possibility. In everyday speech we not only indicate that things are possible, we often state that they are possible in a certain way. Philosophers sometimes speak of three kinds of possibility:

> Logical possibility
> Empirical possibility
> Technical possibility

In ordinary parlance we add sub-categories to this list in a seemingly endless fashion. We speak of historical possibilities, political possibilities, economic possibilities, and we use these adjectives to modify the other alethic terms as well, and thus speak of historical impossibilities, economic necessities, and so on. Under warrant statement analysis we can provide for kinds of possibility (or necessity, or impossibility) by the same device that was used for dealing with kinds of certainty. We employ a warrant component of the following form:

$$\underline{\text{(There are adequate grounds available of a kind } \theta \text{ for)}}$$
$$|$$
$$\text{warrant component}$$

(*d*) Degrees of Possibility. Along with talking about kinds of possibility we also speak of degrees of possibility using such phrases as: slightly possible, virtually impossible, quite possible, and so on, through endless gradations. Once more we have a parallel with certainty statements that can be handled by the same strategy. We merely enrich the warrant component to include a reference to degrees of evidential backing:

$$\frac{\text{There are } \phi \text{ grounds of } \theta \text{ kind available for}}{\text{warrant component}}$$

Through the use of this warrant component we can give a warrant statement analysis of alethic modal statements that provides for all those characteristics shared with certainty statements.

12. THE DISTINCTIVE CHARACTER OF THE ALETHIC MODALITIES

Thus far I have been emphasizing the similarities between alethic statements and certainty statements in order to show that warrant statement analysis is at least generally applicable to alethic modalities. In this section I shall discuss the distinctive character of alethic modalities and make some tentative suggestions concerning how a pattern of analysis can be developed to take it into account as well.

We can begin by comparing an E certainty statement with a corresponding E alethic statement:

(1) It is certain that there is no life on Mars.
(2) Life on Mars is impossible.

Although intuition is not an accurate judge on these matters, it does seem safe to say that the second statement entails the first: if life on Mars is impossible, then there is certainly no life on Mars. But the inference in the other direction plainly fails; it could be an absolute certainty that there is no life on Mars, yet not be true that life on Mars is an impossibility.

The same difference can be brought out in these contrasting statements:

(1) It is impossible *that* Mars supports life.
(2) It is impossible *for* Mars to support life.

While there may be differences in nuances, (1) is close in meaning to the assertion 'It is certain that Mars does not support life', but (2) seems somehow very different, for while (2) entails (1), the entailment does not seem to hold in the opposite direction. The following situation is at least possible: some seventy million years ago every trace of life on Mars was destroyed in an inter-galatal war, and to this day it has not re-emerged. We might, then, have such strong observational evidence in behalf of the claim that there is no life on Mars that we are willing to employ the E warrant statement: 'It is impossible that Mars supports life.' Yet on the very same base of information we might be willing to say that is entirely possible *for* Mars to support life—if we were to scatter poppy seeds on its surface, flowers would soon bloom in profusion.

Generalizing from this single case, we may try to mark out a difference in the following way: in (1) there are no special restrictions concerning the *kind* of evidence needed to establish the material component, but in (2) the cited reasons must have a special character. They must exhibit the fact described in the material component as the result of certain persistent features on Mars. Given the persistent features of Mars (i.e. those that are considered essentially stable) together with causal laws governing the sustenance of life, it must follow that Mars does not support life. In order to capture the force of statement (2) we will need a complex warrant component:

$$\left(\begin{array}{l}\text{There are adequate grounds pertaining to the persistent}\\\text{features of Mars, which together with causal laws yields the}\\\text{result that}\end{array}\right)$$

warrant component

I will not pretend that this warrant component is anywhere near satisfactory, for it is at once too vague and too narrow. At least three items demand further elucidation: persistent features, causal law, and result. The warrant component is too narrow because it does not provide for the alethic force of statements that do not involve causal relationships. A mathematical statement will illustrate this:

It is impossible for a triangle to be equiangular without being equilateral.

Here we would say that the reasons have reference to *defining characteristics* instead of persistent features, and while we could also describe the material component as the result of the application of laws, the laws in question would not have a causal

46

character. We seem to be left with the unsatisfactory conclusion that the warrant component needed for the analysis of alethic modal statements must somehow invoke material reasons that (1) refer to essential features of the subject of the material component, and (2) refer to laws in virtue of which the fact can be shown to follow from these essential features and the laws. This suggestion generates more problems than it solves, but it does outline a programme for applying warrant statement analysis to alethic modalities through an elaboration of the warrant component.

13. A PARODY

Two philosophers, Dr. M. and Dr. S., overhear an astronomer saying that life on Mars is possible. Since they both grant that the astronomer is an expert on these matters, neither wishes to challenge the truth of this remark, but as philosophers they have a desire to *explicate* it. Dr. M., a man of rigid inflexible orthodoxy, reasons as follows:

'The astronomer has really asserted two things: (1) there is life on Mars, and (2) this life is possible. We can set aside the first half of his remark as philosophically uninteresting, but what are we to make of the second part? In the first place we can be sure that we can find nothing in experience that corresponds to possibility so it must be a non-empirical or *a priori* notion. Secondly, if life on Mars was not possible, then it would not exist at all, hence possibility is one of the basic conditions of existence—it's one of the fundamental ontological categories. In summary, possibility is a fundamental trait of existence that we apprehend through *a priori* means. The astronomer is asserting that life on Mars possesses this trait of existence.'

Now to Dr. S., a careless sceptic:

'The first part of your analysis is correct, the astronomer is asserting two things, first that there is life on Mars, and secondly, that this life is possible; and furthermore, you are correct in claiming that possibility is not an empirical concept. But from these facts you draw utterly wrong conclusions. Notice that the claim that something is possible adds not one shred of verifiable information about it. Look at that desk over there;

suppose that I now tell you that it is possibly over there, what additional information about the desk have I imparted to you? Your claim that possibility is a fundamental ontological category is utterly misguided. Possibility is not a descriptive category at all. What then is the force of the term "possible"? I think the simplest and least mysterious account of the matter is this: terms like "possible" and "necessary" provide us with a way of *expressing* our feelings of confidence. The force of such words is emotive, not descriptive; thus the astronomer is making a straightforward assertion and accompanying it with a relatively weak ejaculation of confidence.'

14. TWO PATTERNS OF PHILOSOPHIC CONFUSION

Though I do not suppose that philosophers have ever argued at the level of lunacy of Drs. S. and M., their debate illustrates what I take to be a number of important philosophical points. The first point is this: the very same philosophic mistake can lead philosophers off in entirely different directions—a misguided metaphysics and a misguided scepticism can grow from the same seed.

Since this is an important point, let me dwell upon it a bit further. Imagine an argument whose premises you take to be true, and whose form you take to be valid, but, strange to say, whose conclusion you take to be false or at least plainly dubious.

$$\text{Valid form} - \begin{cases} \begin{array}{l} \text{Pr.} \\ \text{Pr.} \\ \cdot \\ \cdot \\ \text{Pr.} \end{array} \end{cases} - \text{True Premisses} \\ \overline{\text{Cn.}\}} - \text{False or Dubious Conclusion} $$

Suppose than no amount of analysis can shake your opinion that the argument is valid; you are then faced with two choices: (1) you can accept the conclusion, and thus commit yourself to a doctrine that you would ordinarily reject; or (2) you can decide that at least one of the premisses must be false, and thus withhold assent to a doctrine that most people would find unexceptionable. Which alternative a given philosopher is likely to adopt will be determined by contextual considerations since in this situation there is nothing that gives priority to one option over the other. In the parody in the previous section, Dr. M. adopted the first alternative, while Dr. S. adopted the second. These gentlemen are, respectively, caricatures of metaphysics gone wrong and scepticism gone wrong.

The parody has a second point: it exhibits a mistake that philosophers are particularly prone to make, especially when dealing with warrant statements. Both Drs. M. and S. employ the following pattern of analysis:

(1) Life on Mars is possible.
(1') There is life on Mars and it is possible.

The analysis is plainly mistaken, but it does bear a striking resemblance to a pattern of analysis that is perfectly correct:

(2) Life on Mars is abundant.
(2') There is life on Mars and it is abundant.

While I do not suppose that any reputable philosopher would *explicitly* offer (1') as the proper analysis of (1), for in explicit form the analysis is transparently foolish, I do submit that philosophers are often misled by the grammatical analogy between statement (1) and statements like statement (2), and hence tacitly assume a pattern of analysis that they would reject out of hand if it were brought to light. It should not be surprising that this charge is difficult to document in a given text, for so elementary a mistake must be deeply hidden to elude detection by the writer himself. Typically, we can only assert that if the writer were not employing this faulty grammatical analogy he would not be saying the sort of things he does say. I offer two specimens of philosophical confusions engendered by this mistake—specimens that I hope bear a marked resemblance to actual philosophical reasoning.

15. IS NECESSITY LIMITED TO LOGICAL RELATIONSHIPS?

The claim that necessity is limited to logical relationships and cannot be a property of matters of fact is a favourite doctrine of the empiricist tradition. Though some of the motives behind this doctrine are quite praiseworthy—in particular, its anti-dogmatic quality—it seems to me that the doctrine is plainly false and thus liable to do more harm than good.

In order to put this question in a slightly different perspective, let me set aside the word 'necessity' and talk about the term 'impossibility'. The reader may resist this shift since it is obvious that we call all sorts of empirical matters impossible, but the shift is legitimate, for to say that something is impossible is just another way of saying that its denial is necessarily the case. The claim now becomes this: the only impossibilities are logical impossibilities, and thus there is no such thing as a physical impossibility. This doctrine admits of two interpretations: (1) It *makes no sense* to talk about physical impossibility (or any kind of impossibility other than logical impossibility); or (2) whenever we declare that something is impossible in some way other than logically impossible, *we have asserted something that is false.*

(1) The plausability of the doctrine under the first interpretation is virtually nil. We quite commonly speak of things being physically impossible and, in Austin's words, 'even philosophers set some limits to the amount of nonsense that we are prepared to admit we talk'. This blatant appeal to ordinary language would not be a suitable rejoinder to a compelling counter theory, but to the best of my knowledge, no compelling counter theory exists.

(2) The doctrine that assertions of physical impossibility (e.g.) are all of them false usually first rests upon a failure to take into account the *contextual setting* of impossibility statements. This failure produces an argument of the following sort:

Q: But isn't it impossible for a five-year-old to swim the English Channel in mid-winter?

A: Not really, for after all, a stray warm ocean current could appear and just whisk him over to Calais.

The dialectician will be at ease in such an argument; the reason: there is absolutely nothing at issue, and hence *there is no contextual setting that lays down the boundaries of relevance.* The debate soon becomes an exchange of ludicrous examples ('It is impossible that the object in my hand is a super nova') and even more ludicrous replies ('How can you even be sure that you have a hand, for after all, sense perception is notoriously fallible').

But if we turn our backs upon this kind of argument and examine instead live contexts, we see at once that the term 'impossible' performs an honest and useful labour. A teacher makes the following remark to his class (and notice, it is not a philosophical remark): 'It will be impossible to get an A in this class without doing the outside reading; your final will consist of an objective examination covering material *not* discussed in class.' Of course, it is logically possible to get an A in the course without doing the outside reading, and there is a finite possibility of attaining an A through guessing, cheating, or extra-sensory perception. But it is important to see that the original remark must not be construed as denying these possibilities: *it ignores them*. And it *rightly* ignores them because they can have no practical bearing upon the business of telling a student how to prepare for the final examination. It will not help to seize upon this question of practical bearing, for this involves matters of fact, and cannot be settled by speculative reasoning.

A condescending objection might take the following form: 'Of course, in everyday discourse we use such notions as impossibility in a very loose fashion. We often say that things are impossible when *strictly speaking* they are not impossible at all. For the most part, this way of speaking is perfectly harmless; but it will hardly do to take this loose mode of discourse as normative for theoretical discourse. Let us speak with the vulgar, but think with the learned.' What are we to make of this expression, 'strictly speaking'? We might note in passing that this locution typically introduces a quibble, but I'll set this aside. Consider the following remark: 'Strictly speaking it is not impossible to get an A on the examination through guessing; the odds are actually $1 : 2^{100}$.' We can easily imagine a context in which this remark would be correct—it is just the sort of thing one says in a class on probability theory. But to say that this remark is more accurate *as such* than the original remark is merely to give priority to one sort of context over another; and it is hard to see the point of this intercontextual rivalry.

Let us try the following experiment: we can imagine a teacher describing the requirements for a course and remarking, 'It's not impossible to get an A on the final examination through guessing; the odds are actually $1 : 2^{100}$.' This would surely be treated as a piece of irony; we can imagine a student saying to himself, 'If the odds are that slim, it *really is* impossible to get an A on the examination through guessing.' This is a perfectly just remark; he is not speaking loosely, for this remark accurately describes the status of guessing as a strategy for approaching the examination.

Of course, if we grant all this and allow people to talk about empirical possibilities, the next step is to allow them to talk about empirical *certainties*, and this seems to run counter to the principle of fallibilism, a principle, by the way, which the author happens to accept. The principle of fallibilism can be stated in a number of ways. In a narrow version it merely comes to this: there is no class of empirical statements such that its members may always be used without qualification. In this form, the principle is directed primarily against the doctrine that we can have immediate and indubitable knowledge of our sense impressions. A more general version of the principle takes the following form: because of the disparity between the superabundance of relevant data and our limited capacity to cope with it, every empirical judgment is inherently subject to revision.[1] This formulation lacks the rhetorical punch of the slogan that there are no empirical certainties, but it has this offsetting advantage, it does not reduce fallibilism to an arbitrary recommendation that we abandon some useful modes of speech.

Before closing this subject, let me mention one other line of reasoning that will lead to the conclusion that only truths of logic are necessary. This argument is grounded in a search for the locus of necessity or impossibility. A philosopher with an empiricist bent will soon conclude that necessity is not a property of objective states of affairs, for we never find anything corresponding to the ideas of necessity and impossibility in our experience of the external world. The next step is to argue that it does make sense to consider necessity and impossibility properties of propositions. Finally, since necessary propositions have to be true, necessity must be some kind of *truth guaranteeing property*; and this leads inevitably to the conclusion that only truths of logic are necessary, for it is only truths of logic that, by their very structure, can guarantee their own truth.

Under the warrant statement analysis we see that this search for the locus of necessity is misguided, for it rests upon a misunderstanding of the predicative use of alethic terms. Under the warrant statement analysis there is no curious property that has to be given a place; it is no wonder, then, that the search for the locus of necessity should prove such a difficult task. When the empiricist

---

[1] The principle of fallibilism as developed by C. S. Peirce is more than a comment upon human frailty; it is one part of a radical revision of the empiricist philosophy.

searches the world for necessity and fails to find it, he usually retreats to some form of nominalistic scepticism. A philosopher who is not wedded to the empiricist ideal may take quite a different course; if necessity is not met with in sense experience this simply shows that it is the object of reason, not sense. A specimen of this kind of thinking is given in the next section.

16. THE ONTOLOGICAL STATUS OF NECESSITY, POSSIBILITY, AND IMPOSSIBILITY

A question such as 'Are there possibles?' is suspicious on the very face of it, but it could have a perfectly innocent interpretation. Either of the following interpretations (which probably come to the same thing), would be innocent enough:

Are there things that are possible?

Are there true statements of the form 'Such and such is possible'?[1]

To these questions we can give an unhesitating affirmative answer and offer endlessly many examples in support of this answer.

But the philosopher who asks 'Are there possibles?' probably has something else in mind. The very grammar of the question suggests that he views it as being logically similar to the question: 'Are there ghosts?' Or to return to an earlier example, he fails to understand the difference in logic between the two assertions:

Life on Mars is abundant.
Life on Mars is possible.

Notice that I have said that he fails to *understand* the logical difference, not that he fails to *recognize* a difference. The problem here is not one of recognition but rather of giving a proper account of that which is recognized.

The theory of warrant statements provides us with a simple means of explaining this difference, and it is worth while to show this in some detail. Given the valid argument:

Life on Mars is abundant.
∴ There is life on Mars and it is abundant.

[1] It is, it must be admitted, hard to imagine why anyone would want to ask such a question.

let us consider the sequence of arguments that is generated by successively replacing the word 'abundant' by the words 'necessary', 'possible', and 'impossible'.

(1) $\dfrac{\text{Life on Mars is necessary.}^1}{\therefore\ \text{There is life on Mars and it is necessary.}}$

Under the warrant statement analysis this argument is formally valid, for the claim 'There is life on Mars' is the material component of the warrant statement that corresponds to the premiss, and the second conjunct in the conclusion is merely a repetition of the premiss.

(2) $\dfrac{\text{Life on Mars is possible.}}{\therefore\ \text{There is life on Mars and it is possible.}}$

Again the second conjunct is merely a repetition of the premiss, but in this case the first conjunct does not follow from the premiss. From the assertion that there are not adequate grounds on behalf of the claim that there is no life on Mars it does not follow that there *is* life on Mars. Here the principle is: a weak warrant statement does not imply its material component.[2]

(3) $\dfrac{\text{Life on Mars is impossible.}}{\therefore\ \text{There is life on Mars and it is impossible.}}$

Again the second conjunct is a redundancy, but this time the first conjunct flatly contradicts the premiss. In this case, the premiss is an E warrant statement, and from it we may infer that it is not the case that there is life on Mars.

I have gone through these patterns of inference because it seems that traditional thought sometimes involves pictorial thinking that tacitly presupposes that all three of these patterns of inference are valid, and not only valid but also revelatory of reality. I am here

---

[1] This remark seems a bit odd, and in the vernacular we could probably say instead, 'There has to be life on Mars,' or something of the sort.

[2] We might also notice that the conclusion is peculiar because it violates the rule of strength. If we are in a position to make an unguarded remark that there is life on Mars, then by saying that life on Mars is possible, we are using a weaker warrant statement than the evidence demands.

thinking of those ontological hierarchies that áre still met with in current philosophic literature:

> Necessary existence
> Existence
> Possible non-existence
> Non-existence
> Necessary non-existence

I am not saying that this hierarchy is nonsensical—it is possible to give it a simple and innocent interpretation. What interests me are the muddles that arise when this hierarchy is misunderstood.

A sure sign of confusion is the use of analytic statements involving these notions as explanations, e.g.:

> There are no round squares *because* round squares possess necessary non-existence.

Notice how the second half of this sentence suggests that there really are round squares in some sense or other; this calls up an image of round squares languishing in a far-off ontological hell. Or take a remark of the following sort:

> Universal World Peace now exists only as a possibility.

This remark is perfectly intelligible provided that we do not conjure up an image of Universal World Peace standing off-stage awaiting its cue to come on. Finally, there is the following notorious claim:

> God exists because He is a necessary Being.

This is an operative sentence in one form of the ontological proof, and since this proof has enjoyed considerable historical fame, it is worth special examination.

17. A PROTO-ONTOLOGICAL PROOF

The ontological proof comes in a variety of forms, and it is not altogether easy to see how these various forms are related. The Cartesian version of this proof depends upon the claim that existence is a perfection and hence, since God is an all-perfect being, He must exist. I shall not discuss this form of the proof.

Another, and I think more compelling, version employs the following move (perhaps in slightly different terms):

God is by definition a necessary Being.
∴ God exists.

The ontological proof becomes compelling if it is stated against a background of an ontological hierarchy of the sort mentioned in the previous section. If we think that there are various *grades of being*, it is only natural to suppose that there must be a very highest grade of being. In short, a confusion concerning the logical status of alethic modal statements in general will support the confusion embodied in the ontological proof.

But if we examine the argument itself—setting aside contextual considerations that might account for its being compelling—we see first that the premiss is an implicit definition of God. In general (and this is of central importance), when a definition is presented, it makes sense to ask whether there are entities that satisfy the definition.[1] Thus if I define a square as a rectangle with sides of equal length, it clearly makes sense to ask if there are any such entities. The peculiar thrust of the ontological proof (and I take this to be the defining feature of the ontological proof) is that it doesn't seem legitimate to ask this question concerning something that has been defined as a necessary being.

The argument to establish this point is elegant. To deny that there is an entity that satisfies this definition of God commits one to the following doctrine:

A necessary being does not exist.

But this, it would seem, is a flat contradiction, for, as the argument runs, the non-existence of a being is sufficient grounds for denying that it is a necessary being. After all, if something does not exist, it does not exist necessarily,[2] therefore, if something exists necessarily, it must exist,[3] and since God is defined as a necessarily existant being, God exists.

[1] This is not true of definitions of proper names since such definitions are acceptable only if the existence of the thing to which the name is ascribed has been antecedently established. But this sort of definition need not detain us, for it cannot be used to establish the existence of anything that has not already been shown to exist.

[2] A legitimate inference from a negative intermediate proposition to an O warrant statement.

[3] A legitimate inference from an A warrant statement to an affirmative intermediate proposition.

A Proto-ontological Proof

Let us unpack the claim that God is (by definition) a necessary being in the light of warrant statement analysis:

God is (by definition) a being for which there are adequate grounds available (concerning his own nature)[1] in behalf of the claim that He exists.

Or to put this in a more perspicuous, though somewhat less accurate, form:

God is (by definition) a being for which there is a proof (concerning His own nature) available establishing His existence.

Now let us return to the essential question: does it make sense to ask if there is any entity that satisfies this definition? The answer is surely yes, and from this fact alone, we see that the ontological proof fails; for notice that the curious feature of the ontological proof is that it rests upon a tacit assumption that the existence of God has been *antecedently* established.

Before closing this discussion let me anticipate two possible objections. It will not help to add further attributes to God, such as omnipotence, omniscience, perfection, etc. Unless these attributes are said to involve the notion of necessary existence they will not provide a basis for an ontological proof. Furthermore, it will not help to argue that the term 'necessary' has some non-warranting use in this context. This strategy fails because the force of the ontological proof depends upon such warrant implications as 'If Wp, then p'. If someone wishes to assign a non-warranting significance to the term 'necessary', he is free to do so; but now he must offer an *independent* line of argument showing that if something exists necessarily, then it exists.

[1] This clause is usually considered particularly important; in point of fact, it carries no *logical* force, though it does create the image of God holding himself in existence, by His divine boot-straps, as it were.

III

KNOWING

IN Chapter II the pattern of a pure warrant statement was enriched to form the following schema:

There are ϕ grounds available of a kind θ for p.

This pattern provides a way of indicating the kind of grounds invoked and it also allows us to specify varying degrees of evidential strength. Now to say that there are grounds available means that somebody (or a group of somebodies) actually possesses these grounds. The thesis of this chapter, to announce it at once, is that the verb 'to know' and the system of words that forms a family about it—the so-called epistemic modalities—function as warrant statements with the distinctive feature that they specify who it is that possesses these grounds. An epistemic statement is a warrant statement with a special kind of biographical content.

There are a great many terms in the English language that express epistemic modalities, but since this is a complicated subject matter, I shall limit my primary attention to the verb 'to know' and deal with other epistemic terms only in a cursory fashion. There seem to be three main uses of this verb that demand consideration:

(1) Knowing that: 'I know that John is living in Vermont.'
(2) Knowing an entity:

58

(a) A thing: 'Harry knows Bucks County.'
(b) A person: 'I know Samuel Beckworth.'
(c) A subject matter: 'Clara knows trigonometry.'

(3) Knowing how: 'Martin knows how to trap wolves.'

I shall eventually argue that the verb 'to know' has the same sense—a warranting sense—in all these uses; but I shall begin by discussing the locution 'knowing that', since its logic is most perspicuous; then I shall use the results of this discussion as the basis for explaining claims to know a person, thing, or subject matter. I shall, however, postpone an investigation of 'knowing how' and treat it under the heading of practical discourse in Chapter VII.

2. THE LOGIC OF 'KNOWING THAT'

Again I shall employ the device of breaking down a statement into an operator and a material component and then ask if it makes sense to treat the operator as a warrant component:

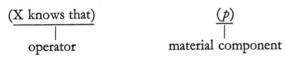

Put in this fashion we see immediately that statements of this form allow for the introduction of negation in two logically distinct ways, thus yielding a fourfold array:

A: X knows that p.
E: X knows that Np.
I: X does not know that Np.
O: X does not know that p.

So far a parallelism with pure warrant statements is maintained.

We may next notice that strong epistemic statements (the A and E statements) imply their material components:

If X knows that p, then p.
If X knows that Np, then Np.

And we can employ transposition to yield the following implications:

If Np, then X does not know that p.
If p, then X does not know that Np.

The first pair of implications embodies the somewhat vague notion that knowledge cannot be mistaken, while the second pair of implications embodies the equally vague notion that a falsehood cannot be known. In the *Theaetetus* Plato recognized these implications and tried—with only partial success—to make sense out of them.

These pairs of implications are sufficient to guarantee that a square of opposition (complete with intermediate propositions) obtains between the A, E, I, and O epistemic statements:

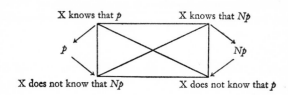

I shall not present the argument in behalf of the claim that this array constitutes a square of opposition since the pattern of reasoning is the same as that employed in previous chapters.

3. A WARRANT SCHEMA FOR 'KNOWING THAT'

Though there are some problems of detail that will have to be worked out later, I shall introduce the following schema for 'knowing that':

X possesses adequate grounds for p.

This schema is like the schema for pure warrant statements save that it provides a way to indicate that a given person *possesses* the available grounds.

This way of viewing knowledge has been implicit in the writings of any number of philosophers, as can be seen by inspecting the following proposed patterns of analysis:

Whenever I say I know, I am always liable to be taken to claim that, in a certain sense appropriate to the kind of statement (and to present intents and purposes), I am able to prove it (John Austin, 'Other Minds').[1]

Another rough group [of parenthetical verbs] is constituted by such verbs as *know, guess, suppose, suspect, estimate*, and, in a metaphorical use, *feel*. This is the group which is used to indicate the evidential situation in which the statement is made (though not to describe that situation), and hence to signal what the degree of reliability is claimed for, and should be accorded to, the statements to which they are conjoined. Thus 'I guess that this is the right road to take' is a way of saying that this is the right road, while indicating that one is just plumping and has no information, so that the statement will be received with the right amount of caution; 'I know' shows that there is all the evidence that one could need; and so on (J. O. Urmson, 'Parenthetical Verbs').[2]

I conclude then that the necessary and sufficient conditions for knowing that something is the case are first what one is said to know be true, and secondly that one be sure of it, and thirdly that *one should have the right to be sure* (A. J. Ayer, *The Problem of Knowledge*).[3]

'S knows that *h* is true' means: (i) S accepts *h*; (ii) *S has adequate evidence for h*; and (iii) *h* is true (Roderick Chisholm, *Perceiving*).[4]

In spirit, the warrant statement approach is closer to the positions of Austin and Urmson than to those of Ayer and Chisholm, but this is a difficult comparison since neither Austin nor Urmson has presented an explicit analysis of epistemic statements. There are two ways in which the pattern here developed differs from those offered by Ayer and Chisholm. In the first place, the analysis as it now stands makes no reference to psychological states (being

[1] In *Philosophical Papers*, Oxford University Press (Oxford, 1961), p. 53. But in the same essay Austin also takes a significantly different line towards epistemic statements when he declares, 'When I say "I know", I *give others my word*: I *give others my authority* for saying "S is P".' This phrasing (unlike the former) suggests a *performative* analysis of epistemic statements, and this suggestion is further enforced by Austin's insistence upon a close similarity between the verbs 'to promise' and 'to know'. Still, as far as I know, Austin never commits himself to a performative analysis of epistemic statements, and I understand that on at least one occasion he verbally rejected it.

[2] Reprinted in *Essays in Conceptual Analysis*, Anthony Flew (ed.), Macmillan & Company (London, 1956), pp. 198–9. I think that it is fair to say that what I call warrant statement analysis is but a working out of one portion of a programme suggested by Urmson in this brilliant essay.

[3] *Pelican Books* (Harmondsworth, 1956), p. 35. (My italics.)

[4] Cornell University Press (Ithica, 1957), p. 16. (My italics.)

sure, accepting, believing, etc.). I shall defend this omission in § 6 of this chapter. In the second place, under the warrant statement approach, neither p nor the claim that 'p' is true is included as an item in the analysis of 'A knows that p', for under the strong interpretation of 'adequate grounds', this item would be redundant (by $Wp \rightarrow p$).

The second difference makes it difficult to show the systematic relationship between the warrant statement approach and Chisholm's approach to epistemic statements. When Chisholm uses the phrase 'adequate evidence' he does not intend it in the strong sense that a proposition is true if there is adequate evidence for it—there can be adequate evidence for a false proposition. Thus, on Chisholm's approach, there need be no systematic connection between the second and third items, i.e. between the adequate evidence that S has for h and the truth of h. I have chosen not to use the term 'adequate' in this way. It seems to me that Chisholm uses the term 'adequate' where most people would use some phrase such as 'thought to be adequate', but I shall not insist on this; I only wish to point out that our proposed patterns of analysis are not nearly as similar as they may seem at first glance. The same remarks hold for the warranting-like phrase 'have the right to be sure' that appears in Ayer's proposed analysis.

The only advantage I claim for the warrant statement approach over the Austin–Urmson approach is that it makes immediate sense out of many of the logical properties of epistemic statements, including all the relationships on the square of opposition presented in the previous section. If someone possesses adequate grounds for some assertion, then there *are* adequate grounds available for that assertion, and from that it follows that the assertion is true. Thus the square of opposition for epistemic statements is grounded on the very same principle that generates a square of opposition for pure warrant statements.

4. A CLARIFICATION

One of the difficulties with the above schema concerns the interpretation of the notion of someone *possessing* adequate grounds. Let me illustrate this by examining three different ways in which a person can be said to possess adequate grounds on behalf of some assertion:

(1) A student has seen the proof of the theorem that the area of a triangle equals $\frac{1}{2}bh$; he understands the proof, and can reproduce it upon demand.

(2) A student has not heard of the theorem that the area of a triangle equals $\frac{1}{2}bh$ nor has he ever thought about it. But if he were questioned about it, he would immediately recognize its truth and be able to offer a proof by drawing upon information he does possess.

(3) A student has learned the axioms and rules of geometry that are sufficient to prove that the area of a triangle equals $\frac{1}{2}bh$, but he has not heard of this doctrine, nor could he, if called upon, decide whether the statement is a theorem or not.

Notice that in each case the student possesses sufficient information for a proof of the theorem, yet we would not be willing to say that all three students know the theorem; we would *not* say this of the third student, and we would be at least hesitant in saying this of the second student.

The third student possesses adequate grounds on behalf of the assertion that the area of a triangle equals $\frac{1}{2}bh$, but only in the sense that he has learned a set of propositions that are sufficient premisses to prove this theorem. We are unwilling to say that he knows the theorem because he is unable to employ these propositions *as evidence* on behalf of it. In order to reflect this demand that the person be able to employ his information as evidence, we can restate the schema in the following way:

X *commands* adequate grounds for *p*.

With this revision, the first and third cases are distinguished and the analysis is brought back into line with common sense.

The second student presents a somewhat different problem. In an obvious way he *commands* adequate grounds for the claim that the area of a triangle equals $\frac{1}{2}bh$, although, to extend this metaphor, he has not *exercised* this command. Now do we want to say that he knows the theorem or not? Here, it seems to me, common sense offers no clear answer; on one hand, it seems strange to say that a person knows something he has never thought about, but on the other hand, we sometimes speak in just this fashion. Teachers sometimes tell students that they do know something, not in an effort to jog their memories but, instead, in order to make them draw an obvious inference from things they already know. If we take these cases at face value, we will be strongly tempted to say that a student can know something he has never thought about.

But suppose we are unwilling to speak in this way, what might we say instead? Probably something of the following sort: 'The second student doesn't know that the area of a triangle is $\frac{1}{2}bh$, but he is able to *work it out* or *discover* it from what he already knows.' This remark does point to a difference between the first and second cases, and where this difference is important we do well to insist upon it.[1] Here I wish only to point out that claims that a person can discover something from what he already knows are themselves warrant statements. One cannot discover something that is not so, although we can try to do this or mistakenly think that we have. A *false* discovery is not a kind of discovery, it is not a discovery at all, just as a fake horse is not a kind of horse but no horse at all.

I think that we are now in a position to settle the issue in the following way: the schema 'X commands adequate grounds for *p*' covers at least two cases, one where we would say that *X knows that p*, the other where we would say that *X can discover that p*. There are cases where we prefer one locution to the other, but there is also a twilight zone where we are hard put to justify the use of one locution over the other. In this twilight zone a distinction can be maintained only by a stipulation that I do not care to

---

[1] Jaakko Hintikka accepts the claim that if we know something, then we know everything entailed by what we know:

$$Kap$$
$$p \to q$$
$$\therefore \ Kaq$$

Here, however, he is talking about *implicit* knowing, a category so wide as to include many cases that we would not call knowing at all. Throughout, he relies upon formal analogies with alethic logic, in this case upon the validity of the following argument.

$$\Box p$$
$$p \to q$$
$$\therefore \ \Box q$$

But by adopting this weak notion of implicit knowledge, Hintikka sets aside one of the crucial features that distinguishes alethic modalities from epistemic modalities, the biographical reference to a person's capacities. Jaakko Hintikka, *Knowledge and Belief: An Introduction to the Two Notions*, Cornell University Press (Ithaca, 1962). See also Chisholm's review of this work: 'The Logic of Knowing', *The Journal of Philosophy*, Vol. LX, No. 25 (December 5th, 1963).

make, since my primary interest is to exhibit the warrant character of statements involving the verb 'to know', and I am not particularly interested in sorting out this kind of warrant statement from others that are closely related to it. So I shall let the schema stand, though acknowledging that it is a bit too inclusive.

5. KNOWLEDGE AND BELIEF

It seems natural to suppose that a person believes what he knows, and for this reason, previous analyses of knowledge have often taken a *belief-plus* form; in other words, the claim is made that knowledge equals belief plus something else. We find this suggestion in Plato's *Theaetetus* where he examines the thesis that knowledge equals true belief plus a *logos*. Towards the end of the dialogue he seems to give up this notion, but most commentators agree that he actually accepts this pattern of analysis and only rejects the various empirical accounts of the *logos* that he has considered. To cite but one further example, A. J. Ayer accepts a belief-plus analysis when he takes as a necessary condition for someone knowing something that he be *sure* of it, and this, I take it, involves believing it.

When such diverse authorities as Plato and Ayer agree on a doctrine, it is only prudent to consider it carefully, and as matters now stand, the schema 'X commands adequate grounds for *p*' makes no specific reference to X believing *p*.

Before going farther, let me make one thing completely clear: there is no systematic difficulty involved in including a reference to belief in the warrant statement analysis of epistemic terms. This could be done easily enough by expanding the schema in the following fashion:

X believes *p*, and X commands adequate grounds for *p*.

In fact, with so much authority on the side of the doctrine that knowledge involves belief, it is very tempting to adopt the above schema and move on to other issues.

But I hesitate to take this easy course because there do seem to be occasions when we can sensibly say that someone knows something without believing it. A belief, to quote C. S. Peirce, 'involves the establishment in our nature of a rule of action, or, say for short, a habit'.[1] It seems that on some occasions a person can know something but still lack those behavioural dispositions requisite for a belief. Perhaps the following is an example of this: Smith knew that he would have an accident if he continued to drive at high speeds, but he refused to believe it. I will not insist that this is a clear counter-example to the claim knowledge always involves belief, but examples of this sort do make the doctrine questionable.

As an alternative to the belief-plus pattern of analysis, the relationship between knowing and believing could be considered *contingent*. Normally, when a person commands adequate grounds in behalf of some assertion this will engender a belief on his part in its truth. But there is no necessary connection between knowing and believing, and on some occasions we find the first without the second. Typically, this will occur when the force of rational persuasion is overpowered by some other force. Since I am swayed by the reasons for saying that the relationship between knowing and believing is contingent, I shall let the schema for epistemic statements stand without including a reference to belief. If the reader is swayed in the other direction and wishes to include such a reference in the account of knowing, he may do so; for whatever decision is made, it will not affect the basic claim that epistemic statements function as warrant statements.

6. PLATO'S SHADOW

... when we are inquiring after the nature of knowledge, nothing could be sillier than to say it is correct belief together with a *knowledge* of ... [something else] (*Theaetetus*, 210a).[2]

This is the last systematic move in Plato's quest for a definition of knowledge, and it seems to leave the inquiry in a desperate state. If the *logos* is not known by the person who is said to possess knowledge, then his knowledge is not grounded on something that he knows; yet if we insist that he know the *logos*, we seem to have generated an infinite regress by eliminating one epistemic claim only to replace it by another. The same difficulty seems to arise for the warrant component 'X commands adequate grounds'.

[1] C. S. Peirce, 'How to Make Our Ideas Clear', reprinted in *Philosophical Writings of Peirce*, Justus Buchler (ed.).

[2] In Cornford's *Plato's Theory of Knowledge*, The Library of Liberal Arts (New York, 1957), p. 161.

If the person does not *know* that these grounds are true, then he will know something in virtue of things he does not know, but again, if we include the demand that he knows these grounds to be true, we are once more off on an infinite regress.

The first thing to realize is that we are here dealing with an infinite regress and not with a problem of circularity. Under the warrant statement approach the original epistemic claim does not appear as a part of the *analysans*, for it appears in a non-epistemic form as the material component of the total warrant statement. More to the point, the *warrant* component contains no epistemic claim about the material reasons. A person can justifiably allude to reasons only if he knows them to be true, but the warrant component does not contain a claim to this effect. Knowing the truth of reasons is something presupposed in invoking them, but it is not something explicitly asserted in the process of invocation.

In answering the charge of circularity, the charge of generating an infinite regress has been conceded. In asserting that we know something we open the way to an infinite process of giving reasons in behalf of reasons. Furthermore, we do not need an initial epistemic statement to start this process, since we need not *assert* that we know something to open the way for the question 'How do you know?' Employing any assertion opens this possibility. In sum, we seem trapped by the ancient pyrrhonistic claim that nothing can be shown to be true by anything short of an infinitely long argument, and hence no one can make good a claim to knowledge.

The way out of this difficulty is not, as some have thought, to find some theoretical device that will put an end to the regress; there are no theoretical limits to the number of challenges that can be brought against a claim. In principle every claim can be challenged—this is another way of stating the thesis of fallibilism —and it is only within the practical context of a given inquiry that the regress sometimes stops. In his brilliant essay 'The Fixation of Belief', C. S. Peirce states this in the following way:

That the settlement of opinion is the sole end of inquiry is a very important proposition. It sweeps away, at once, various vague and erroneous conceptions of proof. A few of these may be noticed here.

Knowing

1. Some philosophers have imagined that to start an inquiry it was only necessary to utter a question whether orally or by setting it down upon paper, and have even recommended us to begin our studies with questioning everything! But the mere putting of a proposition into the interrogative form does not stimulate the mind to any struggle after belief. There must be a real living doubt, and without this all discussion is idle.

2. It is a very common idea that a demonstration must rest on some ultimately and absolutely indubitable propositions. These, according to one school, are first principles of a general nature; according to another, are first sensations. But in point of fact, an inquiry, to have that completely satisfactory result called demonstration, has only to start with propositions perfectly free from all actual doubt. If the premisses are not in fact doubted at all, they cannot be more satisfactory than they are.

3. Some people seem to love to argue a point after all the world is fully convinced of it. But no further advance can be made. When doubt ceases, mental action on the subject comes to an end; and, if it did go on, it would be without purpose.[1]

It is important to see what Peirce is not saying. He is not recommending a very crude version of the pragmatic theory of truth, for he is not saying that a proposition is true if no one in fact doubts it.[2] Nor is he saying that there exists a given set of propositions that are not doubted and that these undoubted propositions form the basis of knowledge. In a way, Peirce's position involves a cheerful acceptance of pyrrhonian scepticism, for in principle any proposition can become subject to doubt, thus, again in principle, every proferred reason can itself be subject to a demand for proof. Peirce differs from the classical sceptics by insisting that the bare capacity to formulate a question by merely putting a proposition into an interrogative form is not sufficient to generate inquiry. At a given time there are formulable questions that no one would want to ask.

How exactly do Peirce's remarks help us in our given problem?

[1] *Philosophical Writings of Peirce*, edited by Justus Buchler. Dover Publications, Inc. (New York, 1955), p. 11. In the future when I refer to pragmatic considerations I shall have in mind just this passage from Peirce.

[2] The pragmatic definition of truth has as one of its unhappy consequences the result that a proposition can be true at one time, untrue at another. Peirce avoids this by defining truth as a limit: 'The opinion which is fated to be ultimately agreed to by all who investigate, is what I mean by truth, and the object represented in this opinion is the real' (ibid., p. 38).

He describes the conditions under which we are willing to use the warrant term 'demonstration', but he does not tell us under what conditions we can *rightfully* use this term. The trouble here is that we wish to bridge the gap between an *outsider* describing features of discourse used in a context of inquiry and an *insider* actually employing this discourse. An insider will accept the claim that something counts as a demonstration if he is shown (to his satisfaction) that it follows from things he does not doubt. A spectator viewing this context will not accept this claim unless he also has these commitments, i.e. unless he is also an insider in the relevant respects.

To return to epistemic judgments, the person who claims to know something does commit himself to producing adequate reasons upon demand, but he does not commit himself to responding to pyrrhonistic scepticism by answering every question that can be generated by converting his reasons into questions. He claims to have reasons that no one will question, but not reasons that no one will ever question, or reasons that cannot be questioned because they are philosophically impeccable. In sum, it would be a mistake to try to avoid the theoretical possibility of an infinite regress of reasons within the very analysis of epistemic statements, for in the first place this will beg the question against fallibilism, and in the second place it ignores the fact that such statements are used in contexts where it is taken for granted that at least some things are known. The sceptic may still insist that we have no right to make the assumption that other things are known, and if he likes he may therefore declare all epistemic statements unfounded. The first part of philosophical wisdom is to recognize that without recourse to pragmatic considerations there is no way of answering the sceptic's challenge.

7. FIRST, SECOND, AND NTH-HAND KNOWLEDGE

The geometrical example used earlier is liable to create a false impression that I would now like to dispel; this is the impression that in order to know something you must possess the expertise to produce a professionally acceptable argument. I know, for example, that a signal cannot be transmitted faster than the speed of light, but I cannot make even a first step in offering a theoretical justification of this claim. What I can offer is a satisfactory argument showing that such a theoretical justification does in fact exist. Now a person who can present a theoretical justification is said to possess *first-hand* knowledge, while a person who can merely argue that such a derivation exists without being able to produce it is said to have second, third, or *n*th-hand knowledge.

The logic of these statements is worth noting. The claim that there is a proof available for some assertion is an example *par excellence* of a warrant statement, and when I claim to know that a proof exists, I am uttering a warrant statement about a warrant statement:

> I have adequate grounds for the assertion that there are adequate grounds for the assertion *p*.

From this it follows that:

> There are adequate grounds available for the assertion *p*.

And from this, the assertion *p* itself follows. Schematically, this inferential chain takes the following form:

$$W(Wp) \rightarrow Wp \rightarrow p$$

In each case, we have a strong warrant statement implying its material component.

We can derive the following expression by transposing the first implication in the above chain:

$$NWp \rightarrow NW(Wp)$$

And this indicates that there is no higher order knowledge without first-hand knowledge, just the result we would expect. In a complex field, such as modern physics, it is sometimes the case that no *single* person can have first-hand knowledge concerning some doctrine, since every individual must rely in part upon the authority of others. Even here, however, we can say that first-hand knowledge exists, though no individual can lay claim to it.

I have dwelt upon this subject in order to avoid an overly intellectual interpretation of the sort of grounds that are invoked by a warrant statement. In our common activities we are fairly lenient concerning what counts as adequate grounds—perhaps too lenient. But it is not my intention to criticize claims to knowledge; I am merely trying to find out what they are all about.

8. KNOWING PERSONS, PLACES, SUBJECT MATTERS, ETC.

At first glance these kinds of knowing seem non-propositional, and for this very reason the warrant statement analysis appears out of place. But imagine a person making the following remark: 'I know Bucks County, but I cannot tell you a thing about it.' The mere fact that a person can tell us nothing about Bucks County is *prima facie* evidence that he does not know it. Thus this kind of knowing is in some way propositional. Still, it is not clear just how it is propositional, for from the claim that Harry knows Bucks County there is no way of telling *a priori* just what propositional information his knowledge consists of.

This last remark may sound peculiar, for surely, if a person knows Bucks County, he knows its county seat. But this isn't so; an ornithologist could know Bucks County without having the vaguest notion about its county seat. Or to take another example, most people who know Bucks County could not list all the precinct leaders of the Republican Party, but we can imagine a context where the following remark makes perfectly good sense: 'We cannot make Smith the party chairman; he doesn't know Bucks County. Why, he couldn't even tell you the party leader in the fourth precinct.'

These two examples suggest a way of dealing with these kinds of knowing, or better, these three locutions involving the verb 'to know': to say that a person knows a thing means that he has *adequate grounds* for making a *relatively wide* range of statements about that thing *which are relevant in some context*. Let me explain the italicized items in this statement. A warrant component (i.e. a *reference* to adequate grounds) is needed since the statements themselves must count as items of knowledge; the statements must be true, but even beyond this, they must be more than lucky guesses.[1] The range of statements demanded is *relatively wide* since in many cases the possession or the failure to possess some single item of knowledge is not decisive in determining whether a person knows a thing. This relativity also provides the rationale behind such remarks as 'Jones knows Bucks County, but Smith

[1] I shall say something about guessing in the next section.

knows it better.'[1] Here we are indicating that Smith is in a position to offer a *wider* range of warranted statements than Jones. Finally, the warranted statements must be *relevant to some context*, that is, they must not be of the sort that can be written off as useless information. The idea of useless information is surely context-bound, for any item of information is potentially useful in some context or other, and thus, claims that someone knows a thing are context-bound as well.

These remarks hardly do justice to the subtlety of the natural language; for one thing, they blur the distinction between *knowing* and *knowing about*. With respect to places, this distinction usually marks a difference between first-hand knowledge and second-hand knowledge. We would hardly say that Harry knows Bucks County if he has never been there; we might, however, be willing to say that he knows a great deal about Bucks County. With respect to persons, this distinction between *knowing* and *knowing about* is much more complicated, so complicated, in fact, that I shall frankly shy away from detailed analysis. Suffice it to say that there seem to be at least two components in knowing a person:

(1) At least some first-hand knowledge of him.
(2) A special personal relationship to him.

The second item, which some may consider the very point of a claim to know a person, falls outside of the scope of warrant statement analysis. This, however, does not constitute a serious problem, for I am not interested in writing a full dictionary entry for the verb 'to know'; I am interested in it only (and to the extent) that it is used informationally.[2] The point I wish to stress is that when the verb 'to know' takes a direct object, sometimes this indicates that we have knowledge of that object, and this constitutes an epistemic use of the verb. My argument, then, is that the verb 'to know' when it is used in this epistemic sense is subject to warrant statement analysis. To use older (and more

[1] There is also a sense in which we can say that someone *knows that* something is the case better than someone else. 'I know better than you do that the Chancellor is irresponsible.' Here, I might mean that I possess more evidence than you do, or perhaps, that my knowledge is first-hand.

[2] It is tempting to say that I am interested in 'wissen' and 'savoir' rather than 'kennen' and 'connaitre', but it seems at least dubious that these distinctions in German and French correspond neatly to the epistemic and non-epistemic uses of the verb 'to know' in English.

candid) terminology, I am suggesting that all knowledge is propositional—a claim of some importance if true.

9. GUESSING

A: I knew that horse was going to win.

B: You did not. You're just saying that now that the race is
over.

A: But I placed a bet on the winning horse.

B: Really? Well, in any case, you didn't *know* the horse would
win, you merely *guessed*.

A: But I felt perfectly confident when I placed the bet.

B: You had no reason to feel confident.

This conversation illustrates that knowing and guessing are
contrasting notions ('You didn't know, you merely guessed'), but
it also illustrates that the contrast is rather complicated.

To begin with, guessing is a kind of performance, although it is
rather difficult to specify just what form this performance must
take. Thus if I say that John did not guess, I can mean two very
different things: (1) that the requisite performance was lacking;
or (2) that it is not correct to consider the performance a guess,
but rather an activity based upon knowledge. We can then say
that the claim that someone has guessed has two components
that are represented by the following schema:

John adopted *p*, and John lacked adequate grounds for *p*.

The second half of the schema is an O epistemic statement, and it
is for this reason that the assertion that someone guessed stands in
contrast to the claim that he knew. But the claim that John
guessed is not the formal contradictory of the claim that he knew,
for it is possible that a person neither knew something nor guessed
it. If, however, the requisite performance is conceded, then the
claim that someone guessed does contradict the claim that he
knew.

In the above conversation the first exchange concerns the requisite performance and is settled by the fact that a bet has been
placed. The last exchange turns on the question of warrant and
illustrates the important point that, in general, questions of knowledge cannot be settled by an appeal to introspective data. I say

in general because on some occasions the relevant data *is* introspective:

Q: How do you know you are sick?
A: I have a raging headache and have felt queasy for weeks.

We sometimes, as in this case, appeal to introspective data as
evidence, but there is no introspective datum that is directly
warranting, that is, there is no introspective datum that guarantees
truth in some non-evidential fashion. Thus, in the conversation,
A's claim that he felt completely confident is simply irrelevant
to the claim that he knew which horse would win. There is
nothing contradictory in the remark: 'A felt completely confident
that Z would win, but he was wrong,' but it is a contradiction to
assert that 'A knew that Z would win, but he was wrong.' The
consequence of this is that epistemic statements cannot be reduced
to psychological statements. It would be possible, I imagine, to
carry on a psychological investigation of the process of gaining
knowledge, but this, it should be clear, is not relevant to our
present investigation.

10. KNOWLEDGE AS A STATE OF MIND

Again, I shall assume that a strong presumption has been created
in favour of the claim that epistemic statements are warrant
statements, and now I shall examine two patterns of confusion
that can arise if this fact is not properly apprehended. Let me
remind the reader that I am not offering an historical thesis; I
shall not assert that philosophers have argued in *just* the way
that I shall examine. I do think that careful textual study would
show that philosophers have employed patterns of reasoning that
embody the mistakes that I shall exhibit, but as stated in the
Introduction, I have renounced the procedure of making historical
claims without historical documentation.

There are all sorts of ways that a philosopher can go wrong if he
fails to comprehend the warrant character of epistemic statements,
but, picking up a notion from the preceding section, the most
natural way of going wrong is to think of knowing as a particular
state of mind. This is a natural mistake because the verb 'to know'
seems closely related to terms that are part of the psychological
vocabulary, including *believing, doubting, suspecting,* etc. All of

these terms have a phenomenological quality about them, and it is easy to suppose that these mental states form some sort of hierarchy with knowing at the top.[1] Notice that this hierarchy of states of minds bears a close kinship to the ontological hierarchy discussed in the previous chapter, and belief in one hierarchy is liable to reinforce belief in the other. Plato, as a matter of fact, presents these two hierarchies side by side in the famous discussion of the divided line.

If we operate under the assumption that knowing is a state of mind, the first thing we will notice is that it is a *truth-certifying state of mind*, for we cannot know something that is false. The first task—and in the long run an impossible task—is to make sense out of a state of mind that is truth-certifying. One way to create the illusion of an explanation is to bring in other warrant terms and use them in place of epistemic terms. We can say that a knowing state of mind possesses the quality of necessity, thus replacing an epistemic term with a strong alethic term, and if the logic of alethic terms is not properly understood this may seem like a sensible explanation. Another device is the use of the vocabulary of perceptual terms in describing the knowing state; knowing is a kind of *seeing*, a seeing that is *clear* and *distinct*. In the next chapter, I shall argue that perceptual judgments are also warrant statements, and hence this pattern of explanation is illusory as well. There is no end to the ways that specious explanations can be produced through the unwitting interchange of one warrant term for another. Under warrant statement analysis we not only see that certain accounts are empty, but we also can make sense out of their apparent plausibility.

There is, however, a much more dangerous pattern of philosophic reasoning that can emerge from a misunderstanding of the warrant character of epistemic statements. This argument starts with a misleading statement of a true doctrine and proceeds from it to a conclusion that most people would find incredible: 'When I know that something is the case, that which I know to be the case *must be* the case. Hence, the very fact that I am in a state of knowing with respect to some proposition guarantees that the

[1] Here we might recall Austin's famous remark about such hierarchies: '. . . saying "I know" . . . is not saying "I have performed a specially striking feat of cognition, superior, in the same scale as believing and being sure, even to being quite sure": for there *is* nothing in that scale superior to being quite sure' (*Philosophical Papers*, p. 67).

proposition is true. Furthermore, this relationship between knowing and the object of knowledge is not contingent; the relationship is analytic since it is plainly contradictory to assert that I know something that is false. But if there is an analytic relationship between knowing and the object known, then the object known must be *contained in* the act of knowing; or to put it another way, in the act of knowing the distinction between the subject and object breaks down. Stating the same doctrine in reverse fashion: if the object of knowledge were distinct from the state of knowing, there would be no way of accounting for the necessary relationship that obtains between them. We may then draw the conclusion that the only thing knowable is mind; and if we are willing to grant the further doctrine that everything is ultimately knowable (i.e. rational), we may then conclude that with complete knowledge, everything would be seen to be mind.'

In the preceding chapter (§13) I pointed out that a philosophically peculiar argument can have two outcomes: (1) it can lead us to accept a doctrine that most people would either reject or find unintelligible; or (2) it can lead us to reject doctrines that would normally be found unexceptionable. The above argument allows for both possibilities. We can summarize this proto-Hegelian argument by the following hypothetical statement:

If there is knowledge, then the object of that knowledge is mind.

If we accept this hypothetical statement we can make one of two moves: (1) we can accept the antecedent, and then through *modus ponens* find ourselves committed to some form of idealism; or (2) we can deny the consequent through *modus tollens* and find ourselves in the camp of the sceptics. Here there seem to be no rational grounds for accepting one alternative rather than the other, hence we are left with a capricious choice between idealism and scepticism.

The initial decision that knowing is a state of mind does not necessitate every step in the above argument, for sanity can reinstate itself at a number of places. We need not talk about a truth-certifying state of mind, and even if we adopt this locution, it need not be given a radically idealistic interpretation. None the less, an important problem remains for anyone who would take this approach; some explication must be given for the entailment relationship expressed in the formula 'Kap entails *p*'. This can easily be done on the warrant statement approach, and I can think of no other way of accomplishing this that is not unsatisfactory in other respects.[1]

II. SOME OTHER EPISTEMIC TERMS

The primary emphasis in this chapter has been on the verb 'to know'; the only other epistemic term that I have considered even briefly was the verb 'to guess'. There are, of course, a great many other epistemic terms (and special locutions involving epistemic terms) that would demand consideration in an extensive examination of this subject matter. I have no desire to enter into such an extensive examination, but I would like to make just a few further remarks that will shed additional light upon the character of epistemic terms.

Perhaps the most common weak epistemic term is the verb 'to think'. The assertion 'I think that John is in the cellar' carries much the same force as the assertion 'John is probably in the cellar'. In each case we are speaking guardedly; we are indicating that we have decent evidence, but evidence that falls short of adequacy. There are also techniques for indicating degrees of evidential strength in more detail; here we often use expressions that seem related to feelings:

> I am quite sure that . . .
> I am fairly confident that . . .
> I have an idea that . . .
> I guess that . . .
> I have a hunch that . . .

We can bring out the warrant character of these locutions if we reflect upon the way we challenge such remarks; for example: 'You don't have a *hunch* that you failed the examination, you *know full well* you did. It was a difficult examination and you studied all the wrong things.' The point of this remark is not to accuse a person of misreading his feelings but rather to

---

[1] With Ayer's suggestion that 'the necessary and sufficient conditions for knowing that something is the case are first what one is said to know be true, and secondly that one be sure of it, and thirdly that one should have the right to be sure', a provision is made for the entailment between 'Kap' and '*p*', but since the first criterion is independent of the other two, the entailment is guaranteed in an *ad hoc* manner.

charge him with refusing to face facts. On close inspection it turns out that *mentalistic* and *feeling* words often have a warranting character, and for this reason warrant statement analysis has a direct bearing upon the philosophy of mind. But once more I must declare this a topic largely beyond the bounds of this work.

A more complicated set of epistemic terms are those perennial favourites of philosophers, 'objective' and 'subjective'. If I say that a report is objective this remark has much the same force as a strong epistemic statement: it would be odd—unless you were an existentialist trying to be odd—to criticize a report because it is objective. On the other hand, it makes perfectly good sense to criticize a report on the grounds that it is subjective. To call a belief (or a report) subjective is to indicate that it is suspicious in a certain way; in particular, the person who holds the belief does so on grounds that are idiosyncratic, i.e. on grounds that are at variance with the common standards of adequacy. Thus to say that objectivity is inter-subjectivity is true, but it is not a great epistemological discovery. It is a truth of logic and nothing more.

There are a great many ways to indicate that the grounds on behalf of a belief fall short of the common standards of adequacy in a particular way. To call a belief biased is to indicate that the grounds on its behalf are defective in one sort of way; through calling a belief naïve, one-sided, pre-critical, dogmatic, pat, unscientific, contrived, old-fashioned, unsophisticated, etc., we indicate other deficiencies in evidential backing. Each of these discounting locutions carries the force of a weak warrant term, but they not only indicate that adequate grounds are lacking, they also indicate in what way (or for what reason) they are lacking.

Finally let me make a remark about 'knowledge'. Knowledge can be defined as the sum total of warranted belief.[1] This is not quite accurate, since there may be things that are known implicitly that no one believes, but the definition is adequate for our present

---

[1] John Dewey has offered a similar definition of knowledge. 'When knowledge is taken as a general abstract term related to inquiry in the abstract, it means "warranted assertability" ' (*Logic: The Theory of Inquiry*, p. 9). There are many places where Dewey could be cited in support of warrant statement analysis, but these citations would prove complicated since the focus of Dewey's attention is the structure of inquiry itself, and not so much the logical character of the discourse employed in inquiry. His, of course, is the more important topic.

purposes. I wish only to note that various kinds of knowledge can be accounted for in the same way that kinds of necessity were accounted for. In each case we do this through indicating the kind of grounds that are invoked on behalf of some assertion. To say that something is a piece of historical knowledge indicates that there are adequate historical grounds in its behalf, just as calling something historically necessary indicates the same thing. I am not, of course, saying that epistemic statements are synonymous with alethic statements: for one thing, epistemic statements carry a biographical content lacking in alethic statements. I am saying that both are classes of warrant statements and that this accounts for both their similarities in logical properties and in tasks that they can perform. It is my hope that these chapters will be mutually supporting through expanding the reader's sense of the personality traits of warrant statements.

IV

PERCEPTUAL TERMS

. . . we prefer seeing (one might say) to everything else.

I shall use this passage from Aristotle's *Metaphysics* as an excuse for placing the primary emphasis in this discussion of perceptual terms on the verb 'to see'. Throughout, the argument will closely parallel the treatment of epistemic terms; in fact, we shall begin by noting three uses of the verb 'to see' that correspond almost exactly to the three uses of the verb 'to know' examined in the preceding chapter:

John *sees that* the dog is on the roof.
John *sees* the dog on the roof.
John *sees how* to get the dog off the roof.

Along with these syntactical similarities—and we could find many more—there is also the interesting fact that the verb 'to see' can be employed as an epistemic term; as often as not, the locution 'thus we see that' introduces something that has nothing in particular to do with sight. Finally, there is the whole range of perceptual metaphors, some firmly fixed in the language, that are used in describing an epistemic situation. We talk about *insight*, *foresight*, and *hindsight*; ideas are said to be *clear* or *unclear*; we *shed light* on difficult problems, etc. This close kinship between *knowing* and *seeing* presumably accounts for the persistent use of visual metaphors in traditional epistemology and philosophy of mind where knowing is often described as a kind of inward seeing.

The Logic of 'Seeing That'

If we restrict our attention to the distinctively perceptual use of perceptual terms, we can say, somewhat tautologically, that the difference between knowing and seeing is that seeing involves a kind of sensing, while knowing does not. How are we to characterize this relationship of sensing? The attempt to answer this question, or a more refined version of it, I shall call the phenomenological problem of perception, and about this problem I shall have very little to say. I shall take the phenomenological aspects of perceptual judgments pretty much for granted, and concentrate instead upon the warrant character of certain perceptual judgments in order to show that a misunderstanding of *this* side of their character can produce troubles in its own right.

2. THE LOGIC OF 'SEEING THAT'

Again I shall use the device of breaking down a statement into an operator and material component, and then raise the question whether it makes sense to treat the operator as the warrant component of a warrant statement:

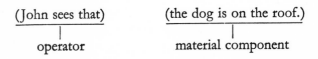

Again it is clear that statements of this form yield a fourfold array of propositions, since there are two logically distinct places where negation can be introduced:

A: John sees that the dog is on the roof.
E: John sees that the dog is *not* on the roof.
I: John does *not* see that the dog is *not* on the roof.
O: John does *not* see that the dog is on the roof.

So far, the parallel with epistemic statements is perfect.
We may next notice that the A and E perceptual statements imply their material components:

A: John sees that *p*, implies *p*.
E: John sees that *Np*, implies *Np*.

Furthermore, the I and O perceptual judgments are implied by the denial of their material components:

I: *p* implies that John does not see that *Np*.[1]
O: *Np* implies that John does not see that *p*.

From these relationships, we may immediately infer that this system of perceptual statements constitutes a square of opposition replete with intermediate propositions:

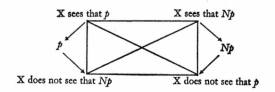

Again I shall not present an argument that this constitutes a genuine square of opposition, since it would be just like those presented in the first two chapters. Here I will only remind the reader of the danger involved in using amphibious statements as counter-examples to the relationships here described.[2]

3. A WARRANT SCHEMA FOR 'SEEING THAT'

Pursuing the parallel with epistemic judgments, I suggest the following warrant scehma for perceptual statements:

X commands adequate *perceptual* grounds for *p*.

In sum, the warrant schema for perceptual judgments is generated by relativizing the grounds to those that are given by sense. We could say that the grounds involve sense data, but this is apt to be misleading since the notion of a *sense datum* has played a variety of roles in answers to the phenomenological problem of perception, and thus it is probably better to avoid this locution altogether.

---

[1] For example, 'If the dog is on the roof, then John does not see that the dog is not on the roof.'
[2] See Chapter II, § 11.

The species of perceptual judgments are dealt with in the following way:

Seeing: X commands adequate visual grounds for p.
Hearing: X commands adequate auditory grounds for p.
Smelling: X commands adequate olifactory grounds for p.
Tasting: X commands adequate gustatory grounds for p.
Feeling: X commands adequate tactile grounds for p.

In each case the warrant component is relativized to a specific kind of phenomenological grounding, and for the reader who cannot recognize these differences, I can do nothing but *commend him to his senses* and hope for the best.

4. SEEING

We can begin the examination of constructions of the form 'S sees x' by noticing one important respect in which they differ from claims having the form 'S sees that x is ϕ'. Tautologically, seeing x involves seeing x, but in seeing that x is ϕ, we need not see x at all. This is brought out by the following examples:

I can see that Oliver has left the room, but in this situation I plainly do not see Oliver.

And somewhat differently:

I can see that a bear has raided the camp, but I cannot see the bear which has long since gone.

Thus *seeing x*, unlike seeing that something is true of x, demands that the person stand in a special perceptual relationship to x. We can symbolize this special relationship by 'πsx'.

How are we to describe this relationship? One procedure is to introduce a third entity that mediates between the perceiver and the thing perceived; the person who perceives x does so by possessing an impression of it:

$$\pi sx = Psix$$

The difficulties with this approach are notorious, for the impression, rather than mediating between the perceiver and the thing perceived, actually seems to cut the perceiver off from the object of perception. To avoid this consequence, it is sometimes argued that the impression (or sensation) is not a *particular* but a way of sensing. Roughly:

$$\pi s x = \text{S senses } x/y$$

One version of this approach has been developed by Chisholm by making the following moves:

> 'S perceives *x*' in one familiar non-propositional use, means the same as '*x* appears in some way to S' (p. 143).

Then:

> '*x appears* . . . to S' means (i) as a consequence of *x* being a proper stimulus of S, S senses . . . ; and (ii) in sensing . . ., S senses in a way that is functionally dependent upon the stimulus energy produced in S by *x* (pp. 148-9).

Finally, with respect to seeing:

> 'S *sees x*' means that, as a consequence of *x* being a proper *visual* stimulus of S, S senses in a way that is functionally dependent upon the stimulus energy produced in S by *x* (p. 149).[1]

It is not far from the mark to describe this as a version of the causal theory of perception where the effect is not the production of a particular in the mind of the perceiver but, instead, a way of sensing on the part of the perceiver—in sum, a causal theory of perception without sense data.

I have taken this brief *excursus* into the problem of describing the perceptual relationship in order to make one thing clear; however important this problem may be, warrant statement analysis will not contribute to its solution. The techniques developed in this work have no more bearing upon the elucidation of this relationship than it does upon the relationship expressed in the sentence 'John is digesting an apple.' Of course, our command of perceptual evidence is grounded in our capacity to enter into perceptual relationships, and thus an account of how we come to have such evidence must wait upon the working out of an accepted theory of perception. But all this falls quite outside the pretentions of this work.

There is, however, one question that does form part of our present inquiry. Beyond the claim that a person stands in a special sort of perceptual relationship to *x*, does a remark of the form

[1] All three passages are found in Chisholm's *Perceiving*.

'S sees *x*' also have a warranting force? The obvious analogy between knowing a thing and seeing a thing suggests that it does, and I think that the following example tends to bear out this suggestion:

(1) A: Can you see that book on the shelf over there?
   B: Yes.
   A: Is it Hume's *Treatise*?
   B: No, it's *Vanity Fair*.
(2) A: Can you see that book on the shelf over there?
   B: Yes.
   A: Who is the publisher?
   B: I cannot tell; I cannot see it that well from here.

In the first conversation, B claims to see something and then offers a piece of information on the basis of his seeing it. The second conversation has a different form: once more he claims to see a thing, but modifies his claim when it becomes apparent that he cannot provide the information requested. Thus seeing, like knowing, admits of degrees. Furthermore, it seems that our assessment of how *well* we see something cannot be decided by mere inspection; before I can answer the question 'How well can you see *x*?' I must have some idea of what is expected of me. In short, in answering such a question, I have to assess my perceptual deliverances in the light of contextual demands. At the very least, statements of the form 'S sees *x*' admit of qualifications that carry a warranting force.

5. APPEARING AND APPEARING TO BE

The closing remarks of the previous section are of slight importance in themselves, but they lead naturally to topics of some moment. In deciding how well we see something we make an assessment of our command of perceptual grounds in the light of contextual demands. Faced with a specific request for information, we sometimes take our perceptual evidence to be completely adequate for giving an answer, while at other times we deem it completely inadequate. But on some occasions our perceptual grounds fall between these two extremes and it is here that weak warranting perceptual judgments find one of their employments. I suggest that when we say that something *appears to be φ* we are asserting that there is at least relatively strong evidence in behalf of the claim that it *is φ*.

Statements of the form '*x* appears *φ*' have quite a different character. I shall call such statements *appearance statements*, and first try to show how they differ from weak warrant perceptual statements, and secondly, how the two sorts of statements are related. As a start, consider the following argument involving an appearance statement:

> The wall appears blue.
> ∴ The wall is blue.

We do not have to turn to philosophy to find a criticism of this argument; it is a platitude of common sense that appearances are sometimes deceiving. In order to make a transition from an appearance statement to a factual claim, we must, as Chisholm has correctly pointed out, supply additional independent factual information, perhaps something of the following sort:

> If a thing that far away appears blue in this light then, in all probability it is blue.[1]

We shall see that the probability clause in this statement will have a bearing on transitions from an appearance statement to a weak warranting statement.

For a moment we can look at another inference from an appearance statement:

> The wall appears blue.
> ∴ Something or other is blue.

Chisholm labels this inference the *Sense Datum Fallacy*,[2] and even though this title is somewhat tendentious, he is surely right in rejecting the inference as one that follows immediately. It is at least possible that this argument could be certified by principles within a theory of perception, but it is hardly an argument that we can start out from when constructing a theory of perception. But setting all this aside, we may notice that a similar set of

---

[1] *Perceiving*, p. 58.   [2] Ibid., pp. 151-3.

arguments can be produced for weak warranting perceptual judgments:

> The wall appears to be blue.
> ∴ The wall is blue.

> The wall appears to be blue.
> ∴ Something or other is blue.

If I am right in saying that the premiss in each of these arguments is a special kind of weak warrant statement, then it is plain that neither conclusion follows validly from it.

Finally, consider this argument involving an appearance statement as a premiss and a weak warranting statement as the conclusion:

> The wall appears blue.
> ∴ The wall appears to be blue.

Again this inference fails unless we invoke a suppressed premiss of the following form:

> If a thing that far away appears blue in this light, then, it is *fairly likely* that it is blue.

Since the suppressed premiss only supplies a fair likelihood that the wall is blue, it becomes appropriate to employ a weak warranting perceptual judgment. In cases where the likelihood is sufficiently high to rule out practical doubt on the matter, we can then derive the conclusion that the wall *is* blue. Thus appearance statements can be used to express the grounds assessed in a warranting perceptual judgment—a fuller elaboration of these material reasons will refer to the independent information as well. I shall return to this topic in § 7.

Appear-to-be statements, like other weak warrant statements, can be used in the formulation of guarded discourse, but there is no reason to limit them to this role. For this reason it would be a mistake to say that they formulate a special kind of guarded assertion. Using a weak warrant statement is not a matter of asserting something yet at the same time not putting our full shoulder (or will) into it. A weak warrant statement makes a full-blooded claim about the status of evidence in behalf of some assertion, and the assertion which, under analysis, emerges as the material component is not asserted at all. It is important to insist on this if we hope to make sense out of uses of weak warrant statements that do not involve the formulation of guarded discourse.

A non-guarding use of a weak warrant statement is illustrated by the following assertion:

The barn appears to be brown, but it isn't.

We are not here giving guarded assent to the claim that it is brown, then in the next breath denying it; this would be rather like saying that I believe that the barn is brown, but it isn't. Instead, the sentence has an amphibious character, in the first half we indicate that the perceptual evidence available from the present perspective lends some strong support to the claim that the barn is brown, then in the second half of the sentence we make the compatible claim that it is not brown.[1] The sentence is amphibious since the grounds assessed in the first part of the sentence can hardly be the same as the reasons that would be brought forth in defence of the second half of the sentence. The non-guarding use of weak warranting perceptual judgments is important, since it will play a central part in the analysis of such troublesome notions as mirages, illusions, and hallucinations.

6. MIRAGES, ILLUSIONS, AND HALLUCINATIONS

Mirages. Everyone would agree that the following argument is invalid:

The horse on the road is a fake.

∴ There is a horse on the road.

I would now like to show it is easy to treat mirages in a way that suggests that this argument, or one very much like it, *is* valid.

Let me begin by giving an example of a mirage: anyone who has driven a car on a road on a hot day has witnessed the mirage of a bright shimmering film of water on the road in front of him. Now suppose that we ask the following question: 'Just what is it that I see on the road in front of me?' It seems natural, and innocent, to say that I see something bright and shimmering on the road. But if I say this, I soon discover that this bright shimmering

---

[1] We can also say that the barn appears brown (i.e. that it has a brown appearance), but that it isn't brown. Again there is no incompatibility, but for different reasons.

something has very peculiar properties. It always stays the same distance in front of me, adjusting the speed of its retreat to the speed of my car. If another car passes me going in the opposite direction and the driver views the mirage in his rear-view mirror, he will notice that the bright shimmering thing is following him, hence the mirage is moving in two directions at once. We could go on compounding such oddities indefinitely.

But in spite of its odd properties, we do seem to be committed to the doctrine that mirages are some kind of entity. It does make sense to say that we *see* mirages, and we seem committed to the doctrine that if we see *x*, then *x* exists. Furthermore, mirages have properties, and some of these are properties of physical objects: they have location (on the road), and visual properties (being bright and shimmering). Some of the properties of mirages exclude them from the class of physical objects, but still, it is a narrow-minded ontology that limits the class of existing things to objects that obey the law of inertia.

We could go on in this fashion and next seek a *locus* for mirages. On one hand, we might place them in the mind—for roughly the same reason that some philosophers place appearances in the mind—or we can put them right out into the public world, and thereby style ourselves as realists. Neither solution, however, is particularly inviting. If we place the mirage in the mind, then we cannot say that two people see the same mirage, and furthermore, it would no longer be true to assert that the mirage is on the road in front of us (unless, of course, the road in front of us is in the mind as well). If we place the bright shimmering object on the road we will have to explain its peculiar, and sometimes seemingly contradictory, behaviour.

Let us go back to the question that started this line of inquiry: 'Just what is it that we are seeing on the road in front of us?' A physical explanation will take the following form: on a hot day the surface of the road is hotter than the air above it, and the air nearest the road is hotter than the air higher up. This gradation of temperature produces a gradation in the density of air, and this in turn causes defraction in light waves entering this layer of air at certain angles. Thus, in most cases, when something appears bright and shimmering on the road before us what we are seeing is the *sky*; the shimmering is accounted for by the convection currents in the air.

Unfortunately, many philosophers would find this physical explanation irrelevant to the philosophical question they are asking: 'When I see a bright shimmering mirage on the road before me I am seeing something bright and shimmering on the road. What we want to understand is the status of the thing seen, and no talk about optics, which yields only a causal explanation, can answer this question.' In contrast, I think that a correct scientific presentation of the facts may be precisely what is needed to get us on the right track in our philosophical treatment of the phenomenon.

Notice that a curious inversion has taken place. When we say that something on the road in front of us is a mirage, part of what we are asserting by this is that we have no reason to suppose that such a thing is on the road before us. Thus, the following warrant statement analysis of mirage statements:

> There are perceptual grounds that we *normally* take to be adequate (or at least quite strong) for *p*, but in this context the perceptual grounds are not adequate (nor even very strong).

I would not insist upon the exact wording of this schema,[1] but I think that it is correct to the extent that it brings out the weak warrant quality of the word 'mirage', for the second half of the analysis contains a weak warrant statement. Furthermore, once we recognize the warrant character of mirage statements, we see immediately that the following pattern of inference is invalid:

> I see a bright and shimmering mirage on the road.
> ∴ I see something bright and shimmering on the road.

Illusions. Illusions are closely related to mirages, and just as we might wonder about the ontological status of a mirage, we might

---

[1] I am not clear, for example, whether the claim that something is a mirage entails that an object of the sort is *not* there. Take the following curious example. I may see a mirage of a lake in just the location where a lake is—this would involve a double mirage of some kind. In this curious setting I could truthfully say: 'That's a mirage of a lake over there, but there is a lake over there.' The decision comes to this: are mirage statements weak perceptual judgements or strong negative perceptual judgments? In either case, mirage statements are warrant statements, and in seeing this we can resist the temptation of giving mirages an independent ontological status.

wonder about the ontological status of an illusion. Consider the famous Müller Illusion:

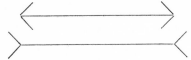

To most people the lower line (exclusive of the forks at each end) appears to be longer than the upper line, while in reality they are the same length.

Notice that in describing the Müller Illusion we correctly use the weak warrant term 'appears'; we have not said that the lower line is longer—in fact, we deny this. We have not, in point of fact, asserted that anything *is* longer than anything else, nor even guardedly suggested this. There is certainly no need to speak in the following way: 'In the world of appearance the lower line is longer, while in the world of reality the lines are of the same length.'

But there are some special locutions involving the term 'illusion' that especially tempt us to set them up as independent entities. Suppose I describe the Müller Illusion in the following way:

The Müller Diagram *creates* the illusion of equal lines having different lengths.

It now sounds as if we are dealing with two distinct things: the diagram on the page and the illusion *created* by this diagram. We can even give a 'proof' that they are two distinct things: the lines in the diagram are of equal length, while the lines in the illusion are of unequal length, hence they are different lines.

How are these two sets of lines related to one another? The word 'creates' suggests that some kind of causal relationship obtains between the two sets of lines, and it is this quasi-causal relationship that reinforces the notion that the illusion is a distinct ontological entity. We are now tempted to draw the following picture of this relationship:

Here the illusion has much the same status as the *idols* invented by the ancient atomists. We can, however, be more sophisticated by drawing the diagram in the following fashion:

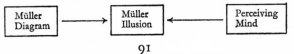

Now the illusion is the joint causal product of an interaction between a physical object and the perceiving mind.

We are now led (under the influence of the above pictures) to the conclusion that we are not aware of lines on the paper, but aware instead of illusory lines located—who knows where? We now think of the second set of lines—the illusory set—as a product of the real set. Of course, we cannot mean this in any literal way since, if we go back to p. 91 we find only one set of lines and it is resting securely on the surface of the page, but still, philosophic reasoning has convinced us that there must be two things present in at least some sense. Why? Because we demand some account of the fact that we see lines of unequal length, when, in fact, the lines are of the same length.

The last sentence reveals the error that has supported this entire line of argument; again the force of a warrant statement has been inverted. When I say that the Müller Diagram creates the illusion of lines of unequal length I am indicating, first, that the diagram presents us with phenomenological grounds that would normally warrant the claim that the lines are of unequal length, and secondly, I am indicating that these phenomenological grounds do *not* support this conclusion. In fact, illusion statements may involve strong negative warrant claims rather than weak negative warrant claims, for from the assertion that the Müller Diagram creates the illusion of lines of unequal length we would normally infer that the lines are not of unequal length. But whether we treat illusion statements as embodying weak negative perceptual judgments or strong negative perceptual judgments, we can still see that the following pattern of reasoning is invalid:

A creates the illusion of B.
∴ B obtains.

The line of reasoning here is precisely on a par with that taken with mirages, but illusion statements are worthy of special consideration because the locution 'A creates the illusion of B' gives special support to the tendency to posit perceptual entities with independent ontological status.

Hallucinations. Hallucinations provide a difficult problem for philosophers who would solve the problem of perception by banishing all mental images from the realm of existing things.

A person claims to see a green patch before him; he can draw a picture of it for us; he can assign it a location in physical space, etc. What are we to say about such a case? Of course, one thing that we cannot say is that the person sees a patch before him, unless, that is, we are describing the situation from the assumed perspective of a person taken in by his hallucination. The remark, 'He sees a green patch before him, but there's none there,' is plainly amphibious. Part of what is meant by calling something an hallucination is that it is not seen by the person suffering from it. Beyond this we are also indicating that he is undergoing a private experience that is very like, and perhaps, to him, indistinguishable from, the phenomenological features involved in viewing an actual object. Until philosophy has done its work, there seems to be no difficulty in being a naïve realist with respect to mirages and illusions, but even at the common-sense level, hallucinations seem to be in the mind and private to the person who suffers the hallucination.

Granting all this, it is still worth while to point out that the following inference is invalid as it stands:

> Jones is suffering from the hallucination that a dragon is after him.
> ∴ Jones is aware of something with dragonlike properties.

Within a given theory of perception this inference might be certified by further principles. The crucial point is that this inference has to be established, and it cannot be used as the starting-point in a phenomenological investigation. Furthermore, until a scientific account has been given of hallucinations, pronouncements about their ontological status are made at a great risk. Recall the case of the mirage. Until a scientific account was rendered we might be strongly tempted to say that a strange entity inhabited the road's surface, but given the account, this temptation was removed. I have no idea what kind of scientific explanation will emerge for hallucinations, but until such an explanation is given, pronouncements concerning their ontological status are, at the very least, premature.

To sum up. A misunderstanding of the warrant status of such terms as 'mirage', 'illusion', and 'hallucination' can generate unnecessary problems within the philosophical problem of perception. In particular, through such misunderstandings we can be led to ontological commitments that are not, in fact, certified. But having said this much, we have yet to offer a positive account of these phenomena, nor, for that matter, have we 'dismantled [a] whole doctrine before it gets off the ground'.[1] The problem of illusion remains after warrant statement analysis has cleared away a few bad arguments.

7. SCEPTICAL DOUBTS CONCERNING EMPIRICAL KNOWLEDGE

Philosophers have not viewed empirical knowledge claims with equanimity; even where open hostility has been lacking there has at least been the feeling that the credentials of empirical knowledge are badly in need of certification. Some of these difficulties have grown out of specific theories concerning the very nature of perception, but these need not detain us. There is, however, a traditional problem concerning empirical knowledge claims that bears directly upon the present inquiry, namely, the threat of an infinite regress. This is the same problem that arose in § 7 of the previous chapter, and I shall deal with it in essentially the same fashion.

In defending a specific empirical assertion we often cite other facts:

A: What makes you think the bird over there is an Olive Backed Thrush?

B: It has a buff eye-ring.

This reply is also subject to challenge; its truth may be questioned (are you sure the eye-ring is buff?) or its force as a reason may be challenged (are you sure that other thrushes don't have buff eye-rings?). I have already conceded the sceptics' claim that there is no theoretical way of placing a limit upon this potential infinite regress. Reason-giving takes place under the pragmatic assumption that at least some claims will not be doubted and therefore not challenged.[2] I have returned to this topic because the problem emerges anew when dealing with appearance statements.

---

[1] This is, of course, the concluding phrase in Austin's *Sense and Sensibilia*, and it refers only to Warnock's attempt to patch up Berkeley's theory of perception. In *Sense and Sensibilia* Austin does not claim to dismantle all the problems of perception before they get off the ground and, for that matter, he nowhere claims to deal with all of the problems of perception.

[2] See Chapter III, § 7.

Suppose we press B in the following way:

A: Are you sure that the eye-ring is buff?

At this point A will probably be at a loss for more factual reasons and instead employ an appearance statement:

B: Well it certainly looks (or appears) buff.

We have already seen that this kind of assertion is not sufficient to establish the claim that the eye-ring *is* buff,[1] for what is needed is a piece of independent information of the following sort:

Things that look buff under these circumstances are buff.

In an apt metaphor, Chisholm describes the relationship between an empirical claim and its support in the following way:

[an empirical claim] . . . is a horizontal structure supported by two posts or pillars—the one post being the appear statement and the other the appeal to independent information. If either post is removed and not replaced, the structure will collapse.[2]

Can either of these pillars be secured against the sceptics' attack by other than pragmatic considerations? The answer to this is, I think, no.

Consider first the piece of independent information:

If a thing that far away looks buff in this light then, in all probability, it is buff.

Even with the guarding clause 'in all probability' the sceptic will find this an easy mark. How could such a principle be established unless we assume in other circumstances the very thing at issue. The sceptic will challenge *any* claim that a thing is as it appears, and if a probability rider is included, he will challenge the assignment of *any* degree of probability. It won't help to lime the thrush and put him right before the sceptic's eyes; for the moment, at least, the sceptic will only admit that the eye-ring looks buff and, no matter how perfect the conditions, he will not accept the transition to 'it is buff'. Hence, the infinite regress. We will, of course, soon reach a point where further questioning is no longer tolerated; in other words, we eventually put our pragmatic foot

---

[1] Even the transition from 'It appears buff' to 'It appears to be buff' demands certification.

[2] *Perceiving*, p. 71.

down. But this is just the move the sceptic wishes to elicit; he wants us to admit that it is only the necessities of life and not the pronouncements of theory that will serve as the foundation of our beliefs. If this is correct, then there is an irreducible pragmatic element serving as the ground for one of Chisholm's pillars.

Does the second pillar also need shoring up in this fashion? Suppose the sceptic challenges the claim that the eye-ring looks buff, how can we answer him? Again it will not help (except on pragmatic grounds) to move the object to a more favourable perceptual setting, in fact, this only invites a new question: what makes one perceptual setting more favourable than another? Anyway, the sceptic is no longer interested in the transition from *looks* buff to *is* buff, he wants us to make good the claim that it looks buff just as it stands. Many philosophers have thought that this challenge can be met, but doing so is a bit complicated. First of all the range of possible mistakes must be limited. To begin with, mistakes about the subject of the looks sentence must be eliminated. If I assert that the eye-ring looks buff, I can be right about the buffiness but wrong in calling the object an eye-ring. Indeed, any commitment concerning the subject of the assertion opens the way for a mistake. To cope with this we can simply do away with the subject altogether by employing a locution suggested by Chisholm:

I am appeared to buff.[1]

Strictly speaking, a grammatical subject remains, but the logical subject has contracted to a *no-ownership I*.

Does the sceptic still have a move to make? I think that he does, for couldn't I fail to appreciate that the colour was buff and take it, for example, to be orange? Couldn't I do this even if I knew the difference between buff and orange but on the given occasion simply failed to appreciate what I was confronted with? Once we recognize the existence of failures of appreciation an opening is made for the sceptic's wedge, for now he will ask us to prove that we have correctly appreciated that which we are aware of.

Once again, a point will be reached where the sceptic's questioning will no longer be tolerated, but intolerance, no matter how

[1] *Perceiving*, p. 62.

strongly felt, does not answer the sceptic. I shall conclude, then, that the appeal to appearance statements as grounds for a factual judgment depend upon pragmatic assumptions in at least two respects: (1) that certain independent information will be accepted without challenge; and (2) that at least some appearance statements will be accepted without challenge. *Warranting* perceptual judgments are used with both assumptions in force, for without them the asserted connection between the material component and the evidential backing could never be made good.

A second, and rather less interesting approach, to sense certainty has been attacked by J. L. Austin. This is the device of retreating to weaker and weaker judgments. In Austin's own words:

> The argument begins, it appears, from the observation that there are sentences which can be identified as intrinsically more adventurous than others, in uttering which we stick our necks out further. If for instance I say, 'That's Sirius,' I am wrong if, though it is a star, that star is not Sirius; whereas, if I had said only, 'That's a star,' its not being Sirius would leave me unshaken. Again, if I had said only, 'That looks like a star,' I could have faced with comparative equanimity the revelation that it isn't a star. And so on. Reflections of this kind apparently give rise to the idea that there is or could be a kind of sentence in the utterance of which I take no chances *at all*, my commitment is absolutely minimal; so that in principle *nothing* could show that I had made a mistake, and my remark would be 'incorrigible'.[1]

In point of fact, this passage contains two suggested routes to incorrigibility; we can call the one the *method of dilution*, the other, the *method of hedging*. Under the first method we make the description more and more inclusive and thereby reduce the range of possible objections. Instead of calling something Sirius, we call it a star; then instead of calling it a star, we call it a heavenly body; then instead of calling it a heavenly body, we call it a physical object; and so on. The limit of this progression is to call the thing a *being* in the widest possible sense of that much abused term. Here incorrigibility and emptiness of descriptive content are approached as the same limit. Chisholm does not employ this technique, and offhand, it is not easy to think of anyone who has, at least in the philosophy of perception.

[1] *Sense and Sensibilia*, p. 112.

The second method, the method of hedging, involves the use of weaker and weaker warranting claims. This is best illustrated by a passage where Austin is discussing some of Warnock's suggestions:

> What Warnock is really trying to do, . . . is to produce, not maximally certain, but a *minimally adventurous* form of words, by the use of which we can always stick our neck out as little as possible. And in the end he arrives at the formula, 'It seems to me now as if . . .' as the general prefix which guarantees 'immediacy', keeps the speaker within the bounds of 'his own ideas'. . . . Warnock's picture of the situation gets it upside down . . . His statements of 'immediate perception', so far from being that from which we *advance* to more ordinary statements, are actually arrived at, . . . by *retreating from* more ordinary statements, by progressive hedging. (There's a tiger—there *seems* to be a tiger—it seems *to me* that there's a tiger—it seems to me *now* that there's a tiger—it seems to me now *as if there were a tiger*.) It seems extraordinarily perverse to represent as that on which ordinary statements are based a form of words which, *starting from* and moreover incorporating an ordinary statement, qualifies and hedges it in various ways. You've got to get something on your plate before you can start messing it around.[1]

Here Austin exhibits a clear case of a confusion arising through the misunderstanding of weak warrant statements. I think other instances of this mistake can be found in the literature, but it is again worth noting that Chisholm does not go wrong, if, indeed, he does go wrong, by making this kind of mistake. Misunderstandings of warrant statements are not the only gates to perdition.

8. CONCLUSION

A full elucidation of the warranting aspects of perceptual discourse would involve a more careful botanizing of the kinds of perceptual terms than I have here attempted. Furthermore, the most difficult features of these terms is their phenomenological character, and except for a few asides, I have said nothing about this. The main point that I have tried to make is that many perceptual terms carry a warranting as well as a phenomenological force, and one of the easiest ways of getting off on the wrong foot in this domain is to fail to recognize just this fact.

[1] *Sense and Sensibilia*, p. 142.

V

THE DICTION OF ARGUMENT

I. INTRODUCTION

THOUGH the families of warrant statements discussed in previous chapters exhibited a diversity based upon the structures of the warrant components, they all indicated something about the status of evidence on behalf of some assertion without actually presenting this evidence. For example, to claim that A knows p is to assert that A commands adequate grounds for the assertion p, but this assertion does not present the evidential backing that A is said to command. In this chapter I shall discuss warrant expressions that do explicitly present evidence. Such expressions are used to introduce an argumentative structure into discourse, and a discussion of these expressions will lead naturally to a treatment of the other lexical features of argumentative discourse—topics that I call the *diction of argument*. The ultimate conclusion of this chapter is that warrant expressions find their primary use as part of the diction of argument.

I can best introduce this topic by means of an example. Consider the following sequence of sentences:

Socrates is mortal.
All men are mortal.
Socrates is a man.

Since I am talking about arguments—and since these statements have been traditionally used to exemplify arguments—the reader will probably treat them as forming an argument. Furthermore, he will probably accept the first two sentences as premises, the third sentence as a conclusion, and declare the argument invalid on the grounds that it commits the fallacy of the undistributed middle. Nevertheless, the reader will probably feel somewhat uneasy, for logicians always use a more elaborate symbolism in representing an argument, something of the following sort:

> Socrates is mortal.
> All men are mortal.
> ∴ Socrates is a man.

Here the bar and triple dot mark off (by convention) the premises and conclusion, and thus introduce the rudimentary features of an argumentative structure—they thus form part of the diction of argument. I shall begin this discussion of the diction of argument by examining some of the more commonplace means for introducing argumentative structure into discourse.

2. WARRANTING CONNECTIVES

To be an argument, a sequence of expressions must meet the following minimal condition: it must be clear that certain statements have the status of premises, while some other statement has the status of a conclusion. This can be accomplished in a wide variety of ways—through gestures, intonation, special typographical conventions—but usually it is done through the use of special conjunctions. To return to the original example, the following use of conjunctions yields quite a new argument:

> Socrates is mortal.
> *Since* All men are mortal
> *and* Socrates is a man.

Or to write this in the normal linear fashion:

> Socrates is mortal since all men are mortal and Socrates is a man.

By a natural extension of the previous terminology I shall call these terms that mark off premises and conclusions *warranting connectives*, for unlike other connectives (e.g. truth–functional connectives) these expressions introduce an *evidential* relationship between propositions. It would also seem natural to call those sentences that contain these connectives a new kind of warrant statement, but as we shall see in the next section, this would be a mistake.

A partial list of terms that often function as warranting connectives will add some substance to this discussion:

accordingly	so
(because)	since
hence	then
thus	therefore

These terms do not always function as warranting connectives, in particular, those carrying a temporal sense have other uses. Furthermore, even when used as warranting connectives, they need not be synonymous; among other things, they have varying grammatical properties; for example, the following sentences introduce reversed warranting relationships:

The dam burst because the flood-gate jammed.
The dam burst so the flood-gate must have jammed.

While acknowledging such differences, I do not propose to examine them in detail; instead, I shall concentrate upon the common properties of warranting connectives.

3. ARGUMENTS AND ASSERTIONS

In the preceding two sections I have quietly dropped the phrase 'warrant statement' and replaced it by the more neutral locution 'warrant expression'. The reader familiar with Gilbert Ryle's important essay ' "If", "So", and "Because",' will guess at the reason for this change; in the list of warranting connectives we find the term 'so', and about constructions containing this connective Ryle has made the following, and it seems to me correct, claim:

... 'Today is Monday, so tomorrow is Tuesday' is not a statement. It is an argument, of which we can ask whether it is valid or fallacious; it is not an assertion or doctrine or announcement which we can ask whether it is true or false.[1]

It seems, then, that warranting connectives are not used in the production of a new kind of warrant *statement* because they are not

[1] Gilbert Ryle, ' "If", "So", and "Because",' in *Philosophical Analysis*, edited by Max Black, Cornell University Press (Ithaca, 1950), p. 324.

used in the production of statements at all—they are used to formulate arguments.

There would be no difficulty in shifting from talk about statements to talk about arguments when discussing constructions that employ these connectives if it weren't for the fact that the list contains one troublesome item, the connective 'because'. Ryle takes the opposite line when dealing with constructions that employ this connective:

> ... 'Tomorrow is Tuesday, because today is Monday' is [a] statement which may be true.[1]

Once more Ryle has accurately reported upon a linguistic habit, but he does not exhibit the ground of this habit; we want to know the character of because-sentences in virtue of which it is appropriate to treat them as assertions. I shall not venture where Ryle has feared to tread. With this decision, the application of the warrant statement approach to the problem of explanation is set aside for another day. I shall concentrate on arguments whose function it is to establish the truth of their conclusion; I shall call such arguments *justificatory* arguments in opposition to another sort of argument that we might call *explanatory*. Virtually everything that is said about justificatory arguments will hold, *mutatis mutandis*, for explanatory arguments, but there are extra problems posed by explanations which I do not propose to discuss.[2]

It will be useful to present an argument (along the lines developed by Ryle) showing that sentences employing warranting connectives express arguments, not assertions. For the sake of a change, I shall consider constructions of the form 'Since p, q'—I think there is a greater temptation to think that such constructions express assertions than there is with Ryle's example 'p, so q'. The same argument could be constructed for any of the warranting connectives listed in the previous section with the exception of the problematic connective 'because', which is often, though by no means always, used in the formulation of an explanation.

When we commit ourselves to 'Since p, q', we thereby commit ourselves to the truth of both 'p' and 'q', and by misunderstanding

---

[1] Gilbert Ryle, p. 324.

[2] I have gone into the problems of justification and explanation in some detail in an article entitled 'Inferential Constructions', *American Philosophical Quarterly* (January, 1967).

the character of this commitment we may be led to the following pattern of analysis:

(1) 'Since p, q' = 'p & q'.

Obviously, this will not do. In the original an inference is made from 'p' to 'q' and this inferential aspect is not captured in the simple conjunction 'p & q'. To remedy this defect, we can expand the proposed analysis in the following way:

(2) 'Since p, q' = '(p & q) & (that p implies that q)'.

This will constitute no advance at all if 'that p implies that q' is analysed as a material implication, for this renders the second conjunct in the *analysans* redundant. Waiving this point we can still note that, in the original, 'q' is specified as the conclusion—we affirm 'q' on the basis of an inference from another proposition we affirm—while under the proposed analysis no conclusion is designated. It will not help to delete 'q' from the *analysans*, thus forcing a listener to draw the inference for himself:

(3) 'Since p, q' = 'p & (that p implies that q)'.

'Since p, q' does not set a logical task that might, after all, be carried out badly; it performs one. Finally, the *analysans* can be expanded in a way that does include the specification of a conclusion:

(4) 'Since p, q' = '(p & (that p implies that q)), therefore q'.

This will hardly do, for we have simply got over the difficulty of designating a conclusion by employing a second warranting connective. On top of this we are now off on an infinite regress, we have generated the Lewis Carroll paradox of Achilles and the Tortoise by including the principle of the inference as a premiss needed in the argument falling under that principle. This, it seems to me, is the dead end of the doctrine that constructions such as 'Since p, q' express assertions.

4. THE WARRANT STATEMENT COUNTERPARTS OF ARGUMENTS

If we treat 'Since p, q' and similar sentences as arguments, not assertions, then the author's favourite device of constructing squares of opposition exhibiting entailment relationships seems

out of place. An argument does not entail anything, nor does anything entail an argument. We can, none the less, construct a
square of opposition for an important set of statements *about*
arguments. I shall say that an argument is *sound* if its premisses
establish the truth of the conclusion. Two criteria for a sound
argument are that its premisses are true, and that the conclusion
follows from these premisses.[1] From this definition we can derive
the following theses concerning the soundness of an argument.

(*a*) If ϕ is a sound argument, its conclusion is true.

(*b*) If ϕ is a sound argument, then the same argument with the
conclusion denied is unsound.

(*c*) If '*p*' is true, then there is no sound argument having the
denial of '*p*' for its conclusion.[2]

These three theses embody the relationships for a square of opposition on which all the standard entailments hold. Using '*S*
"since *p*, *q*"' as an abbreviation for '"since *p*, *q*" expresses a sound
argument', we can construct the following square of opposition.

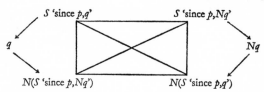

As already conceded, there can be no warrant statement analysis
of sentences such as 'since *p*, *q*', for such sentences do not express
statements. We can, however, adopt a warrant statement analysis
of these claims about soundness, and thereby provide for the
familiar square of opposition. The move here should be obvious:

'that *p* warrants that *q*' = '*S* "since *p*, *q*"'

(The idea of one proposition warranting another is richer than
the idea of one proposition entailing another, for saying that one

---

[1] We might also insist that the conclusion follow relevantly and non-circularly
from the premisses, and even beyond this, we may want to include pragmatic features
in the full definition of soundness. For an argument to be sound (i.e. for it to
establish its conclusion, the premisses must be *known* to be true by those engaged in
the argument, and that the conclusion follows from the premisses must be *apparent*
to them. I have neglected these pragmatic features only because they will not be
needed in the argument I shall develop.

[2] This same set of theses will not hold for the *validity* of an argument, for we can
have a valid argument with a false conclusion.

proposition entails another does not commit one to the truth of the consequent.) Dropping the *thats* in the standard abbreviational manner, we can now construct a square of opposition for a new system of warrant statements:

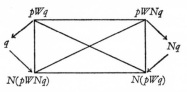

This square is generated by holding '*p*' constant throughout. Quite another square emerges if we hold '*q*' constant and allow '*p*' to vary. This second square is related in interesting ways to explanatory arguments (arguments where the truth of the consequent is not normally at issue), but this area has been declared out of bounds.

To sum up. In an argument we *present* one proposition (or a set of propositions) as the warrant for another. In doing this we are dealing with assertions, but we are not relating them in a fashion that yields one larger compound assertion. With warrant statements of the form 'that *p* warrants that *q*' we *assert* that a warranting relationship holds between propositions. Since in one case we are asserting while in the other we are not, these two kinds of discourse will never meet at the level of analysis. None the less, such warrant statements display the central feature of an argument and thus can be useful for their elucidation.

5. MATERIAL REASONS

A warranting connective statement (i.e. any statement of the form 'that *p* warrants that *q*') states that a given assertion (the antecedent) supplies adequate grounds for a further assertion (the consequent). If we employ the standard device of breaking a warrant statement into two components—a material and a warrant component—we again have an instance of a strong warrant statement entailing its material component.

$$p W \qquad\qquad q$$

| warrant | material |
| component | component |

$$(pWq) \text{ entails } q$$

If a specific proposition warrants '*q*', the '*q*' is warranted, and, of course, if '*q*' is warranted, it is true; for this reason the material component plays the role of an intermediate proposition in the square of opposition.

The warrant component of a warranting connective statement differs from our previous warrant components in that it not only indicates the status of evidential backing, it actually includes a reference to a piece of evidence. To mark off this distinctive feature, we shall divide the warrant component into two further parts and label them as follows:

$$p \qquad W$$

material	warranting
reason	connective

We can now raise the important question: what is the relationship between the material reason[1] and the material component in a true warranting connective statement?

For one proposition to warrant another, the first must be true and the second follow from it, thus in a warranting connective statement, the material reason must be true and the material component must follow from it. What are we to make of this idea of one proposition following from another? If we turn to logicians for help on this matter we find that they speak with many voices. One area of controversy, and there are many, centres on the notion of relevance. In older logic texts we find the doctrine that one proposition can follow from another only if the latter is relevant to the former, but many contemporary logicians have seen fit to set aside this demand for relevance in their definitions of entailment and implication. Relevance, it seems, is not relevant to logic. There is, however, nothing like unanimity on this matter; any number of attempts have been made to find a theory of entailment that captures the ideal of relevance; unfortunately, those logicians who accept the demand for relevance are nowhere near agreement on how it should be met. Now it should be obvious that the relationship between the material reason and the material component in a warranting connective statement must involve the notion of relevance; it will hardly do to have one proposition warrant another while at the same time be irrelevant to it. Thus a

---

[1] A notion first introduced in Chapter I, § 7.

full treatment of warranting connective statements (and the arguments to which they correspond) must wait upon the development of an acceptable theory of relevance. For the remainder of this discussion I shall simply take it for granted that the demand for relevance is met, however this is accomplished.

With the problem of relevance swept under the rug, we can again ask the question: what are we to make of this idea of one proposition following from another? Certainly the demand that the material reason *logically* entail the material component is much too stringent—under this demand virtually every argument that occurs in common parlance would be unsound and every corresponding warranting connective statement false. At the very least, we must retreat to the demand that the material reason *enthymematically* entail the material component, i.e. that the material reason together with true suppressed premisses logically entail the material component. The strength of this restriction will depend upon what can be admitted as a suppressed premiss; logicians are usually niggardly on this matter, allowing only such things as logical truths about relations, while the plain man seems to admit anything provided that it is well known and naturally suggests itself in the context of the argument. (Of course, the plain man doesn't have a theory about enthymemes, but he seems to adopt this principle in his assessments of arguments.) A logician will resist this permissive attitude towards suppressed premisses because it relativizes the notion of a sound argument to the knowledge of people engaged in arguing; and he is right in thinking that such considerations have no place in formal logic, but they do have a place in an investigation of what is normally involved in saying that one proposition follows from another.

We should also make a nod in the direction of inductive inferences, for we sometimes say that one proposition follows from another if the second provides strong inductive evidence for the first. Finally, there is a style of argument that is often used but rarely discussed in logic texts. We sometimes agree that '*p*' follows from '*q*' provided that '*q*' lends some strong support to '*p*' and *that all objections to '*p*' have been rebutted*. The difficulty with this procedure is that there is normally no effective procedure for hunting down all potential objections and hence there is always a possibility (usually a live possibility) that some sound objection has been overlooked. This is something like the risk that we run in maintaining an inductive generalization where there is always a possibility of turning up a counter-instance, but with an inductive generalization we at least know in advance what will count as strong counter-evidence; in defending a rich thesis via the method of discounting objections, a refutory argument may come from the blue.[1]

A philosopher with a rationalist bent may deplore the use of arguments that lean heavily upon the strategy of discounting objections—perhaps we can say that rigour varies inversely in proportion to the density of discounting arguments used—but the point here is to describe some of the standard canons we employ in assessing a move from premises to a conclusion, not to criticize them.

6. THREE MORE CATEGORIES OF THE DICTION OF ARGUMENT

Thus far I have only discussed the use of warranting connectives for marking off premises and conclusions; and warranting connectives are the ∴ of common parlance. I shall now discuss three other important jobs performed by warrant expressions in reasoned discourse: *assuring, guarding,* and *discounting.*

Assuring. The idea that no assertion is to be accepted unless a sound argument is brought forward in its defence has this

---

[1] Nuel Belnap has suggested an ingenious method of converting these discounting arguments into a form of inductive reasoning. If we interpret the claim that there are no objections to a proposition as meaning that there are no true propositions that entail its denial, we can produce the following argument:

$$(1) \sim (\exists q)[q \ \& \ (q \to \ \sim p)]$$
$$(2) \ (q)[\ \sim q \lor \ \sim (q \to \ \sim p)]$$
$$(3) \sim (\sim p) \lor \ \sim (\sim p \to \ \sim p)$$
but
$$(4) \ \sim p \to \ \sim p$$
$$(5) \sim (\sim p)$$
so
$$(6) \ p$$

Thus if there is no objection to a proposition (under this interpretation of an objection) then the proposition is true, so in meeting objections we are lending support to a proposition that entails the conclusion we wish to establish.

There are, however, some difficulties with this. We might want to reject the initial interpretation of the claim that there are no objections to the truth of a proposition and we might also challenge step (4) by not accepting the principle that every proposition entails itself. Finally, we would have to face up to the paradox of confirmation, for in showing that any *arbitrary* true proposition does not entail the denial of our conclusion we would be lending inductive support to our conclusion. Faced with the elegance of the argument on one hand and the objections on the other, I'm afraid that I do not know what to say.

embarrassing consequence: it leads us off into an infinite regress of arguments should we ever attempt to establish a single doctrine. There is a genuine philosophical problem here: it seems dogmatic to accept an assertion without a sound argument being brought forward in its behalf, but if we don't become dogmatic at some point, the infinite regress will surely arise. Sceptics thrive on arguments of this sort, for what grounds, they ask, do we have for selecting our dogmatism over another; any argument in favour of a particular dogmatism will simply initiate another infinite regress which can only be stopped by yet another dogmatic appeal.

This pyrrhonistic puzzle has its practical counterpart in the problem of presenting a sound argument. Any reason that is brought forward is itself subject to challenge, and in meeting this challenge we are apt to open ourselves to even further challenges. To avoid such challenges we employ two basic strategies: wherever possible we try to offer as reasons statements that are matters of common consent; failing this, we offer assurances that we are able to defend those statements that are apt to be challenged. If people habitually challenged every statement that they found the least bit dubious, assurance giving would serve no function, but the efficient use of language depends upon a degree of mutual trust, and assurance giving relies upon this fact.

In giving assurances we often appeal to authority: 'doctors agree', 'history has shown', 'common sense tells us', 'the great minds of all ages concur', etc. Statements that make such an appeal to authority have the status of strong warrant statements, for in appealing to authority we are not merely citing a statistical fact (doctors *happen* to agree that); we are stating that those people who command adequate information concur, and this amounts to saying that there are adequate grounds on behalf of the claim that is made. *In fact, the whole system of strong warrant statements finds its chief employment in the business of giving assurances.* This point was made earlier (Chapter I, § 7), but I shall repeat it: in giving assurances we indicate that we are speaking in a serious and considered fashion, and by giving such a pledge we can often protect our remarks from criticism.

Guarding. A guarded statement is more easily defended (since it commits us to less) than an unguarded discourse, and thus by guarding our premises we can make them less subject to criticism. Weak warrant statements (especially the stronger ones) find their chief employment in formulating guarded statements embodying such locutions as: 'it is possible that', 'it is probable that', 'it may be that', 'I think', 'I suppose', 'it seems to be', 'it looks as if', 'it sounds as if', 'it appears to be', etc.

Guarding, unlike assuring, is a double-edged sword, for while it supplies us with a way of protecting our assertions, it does so at the price of weakening what we say. A guarded premiss is less subject to criticism, but it also offers less support for the conclusion. Guarding, in fact, produces the most persistent and the most difficult problem for the assessment of informal arguments. How much support does this set of guarded premisses give to the conclusion? This is one of the basic questions of practical logic.

Discounting. I shall call the process of attacking an argument 'discounting', a procedure that can be used in criticizing the conclusions of others or, as we saw in the previous section, for establishing a conclusion of our own via the method of rebutting objections. Discounting can involve any one of three moves:

(1) Grant the truth of the premisses, but deny the inference from them.
(2) Grant the validity of the inference, but deny the truth of the premisses.
(3) Deny both the truth of the premisses and the validity of the inference.

The English language provides a rich battery of locutions that perform these discounting jobs, and I can give only a small sampling of the locutions employed under each of these headings.

(1) The first sort of discounting is illustrated by the following remarks:

The ring is beautiful but expensive.
The ring is expensive but I'll still buy it.

When the word 'but' is used as a connective, it has the truth–functional force of a conjunction (a remark of the form '*p* but *q*' is acceptable only if both '*p*' and '*q*' are true); however, the *distinctive* force of the word 'but' is that it discounts potential implications of that which precedes it. Consider the first remark, 'The ring is beautiful but expensive.' In most contexts the claim that the ring is beautiful would count as a favourable comment (giving, for example, *a* reason for choosing it), while the continuation, 'but expensive', discounts this favourable comment and gives the entire sentence unfavourable force. A person who rejects a ring because it is beautiful but expensive not only gives a reason for rejecting it (it's expensive), he also makes it clear that he has considered the ring's beauty in coming to his decision. He thus anticipates any defence of the ring on the grounds of its beauty.

The second remark, 'The ring is expensive but I'll still buy it,' has a different structure. Here a decision is defended by discounting a possible objection to this decision. Notice that no reason is given for discounting the ring's expense as a ground for rejecting it, but once more the mere fact that a possible objection has been acknowledged creates the presumption that it was not ignored in the overall assessment. Sometimes a statement will combine the features of both these remarks and not only discount an objection to a possible decision but also give a reason on behalf of this discounting, for example, 'Although the ring was beautiful, I did not buy it since it was too expensive.' This sentence employs both a discounting term, 'although',[1] and a warranting connective, 'since', and through this combination of terms a reason is given and a possible objection discounted.

In logical character the discounting terms bear a close kinship to the I and O propositions on the square of opposition for warranting connective statements. In this mode of discounting we indicate that one proposition that we accept does not warrant the denial of another proposition that we accept. Symbolically, we can characterize this pattern of discounting by the two following expressions:

$$(p \ \& \ (q \ \& \ (N(qWNp)))) \qquad (Np \ \& \ (q \ \& \ (N(qWp))))$$

Here the I and O warranting connective statements appear as the innermost conjunct of the respective larger warrant statements.

I shall call those terms that perform this kind of discounting 'discounting connectives'—the intended parallel with warranting connectives should be obvious. Earlier we saw that sentences employing warranting connectives did not express assertions but arguments instead, and for that reason were not subject to a warrant statement analysis. What are we to say about sentences employing discounting connectives, do they express assertions or

---

[1] Notice that the term 'although' (unlike the term 'but') discounts that which follows it.

not? Certainly when we say that a ring is beautiful but expensive we commit ourselves to the truth of the propositions 'The ring is expensive' and 'The ring is beautiful' just as there is a like commitment in saying that the ring is expensive since it is beautiful. But it seems that in both cases we miss the point of the remark if we render them as conjunctive assertions: a warranting connective provides a way of arguing, i.e. of affirming one proposition *on the basis* of another that we affirm; a discounting utterance has the reverse function, it allows us to affirm a proposition *in the teeth* of another proposition that we affirm. It would seem that *affirming on the basis* of and *affirming in the teeth* of are on a par in this respect, neither move can be captured in an *analysans* that is purely assertive. I shall conclude, then, that there can be no warrant statement analysis of sentences employing discounting connectives; at best we can construct warrant statement counterparts for such constructions.

An examination of sentences containing warranting connectives and discounting connectives together with their warrant statement counterparts, exhibits an interesting application of the rule of strength:

Originals	Warrant statement counterparts
(a) Since p, q	(a') pWq
(b) q, although p	(b') q & $(p$ & $N(pWNq))$

Notice that (a') entails (b') but not conversely, thus the use of (b') where (a') can legitimately be used represents a violation of the rule of strength. There are no entailment relationships between (a) and (b), but the rule of strength applies to them none the less. Imagine someone saying 'q, although p' in a context where he could legitimately say 'since p, q'; what objection can we bring against him? We cannot criticize him on the grounds that either 'p' or 'q' are false, nor on the ground that 'p' does in fact refute 'q' (both apt criticisms in some contexts), for in accepting 'since p, q', we have ruled out these criticisms. Instead, we can accuse him of a grotesque violation of the rule of strength: 'What do you mean, the generator is working although the light is on; since the light is on the generator *must* be working.'[1] The foundation for this application of the rule of strength is revealed by inspecting the

---

[1] The word *must* (spoken with special emphasis) underscores the legitimacy of the inference.

logical relationships between the respective warrant statement counterparts.

A partial list of terms that function as discounting connectives includes the conjunctions:

although	none the less
but	though
however	still
nevertheless	yet

It should go without saying that these conjunctions do not always function as discounting connectives, and even when they do function in this way they need not be synonymous, for at the very least some of them exhibit different grammatical properties.

(2) In the second mode of discounting mentioned on p. 110 we grant the validity of an argument, but discount it on the grounds that the premiss is false. In other words, we say something of the following sort: 'If such and such *were* true, then so and so *would be* true, but such and such isn't true.' Once more the job of discounting is involved by the use of the term 'but'; none the less, this discounting is implemented by the use of the subjunctive mood, here indicating that the antecedent is *contary to fact*, i.e. false. Thus, through the use of the subjunctive we can acknowledge that an implication holds but at the same time discount it on the grounds that the requisite antecedent is false. Once more, if we are defending a position rather than merely attacking another's, this allows us to indicate that our reasoning has not been carried out in ignorance of a potential criticism.

(3) In the third mode of discounting we concede nothing; we reject a reason as false, and deny an inference from it. We may say something of the following sort: 'Even if the ring were beautiful, I still would not buy it.' Basically, this remark discounts beauty as a reason for buying the ring; at the same time, however, it discounts the claim that the ring is beautiful. This is a piece of double discounting. And again, through the use of this discounting expression we can either attack a position or defend ourselves through indicating that our own decision was not made without reference to a potential criticism.

In point of fact, any warrant statement can be given a discounting role. An I warrant statement discounts a claim that a negative statement is warranted, and an O warrant statement discounts a claim that an affirmative statement is warranted. The A and E warrant statements mutually stand in the strongest possible discounting relationship.

It would seem that in the area of criticism—levelling criticism, anticipating criticism, answering criticism, etc.—warranting expressions bloom in the richest imaginable profusion. Rather than try to list a whole string of terms that carry a warranting force, let me simply suggest that the reader attend to the language of argumentation; to the way in which arguments are put together, attacked, and defended. All of the warrant terms discussed in these five chapters will be found at work, but endlessly many more as well.

7. CONCLUSION TO PART ONE

The initial definition of a warrant statement took the following form: 'A warrant statement is any statement that indicates something about the status of the evidential backing available for some further statement,' and in the first four chapters I have tried to give some indication of the wide range of statements that can be subsumed under this definition. In this chapter I have applied the warrant statement approach to constructions that do not express assertions and I have tried to exhibit their warrant character by comparing them with warrant statement counterparts. I have concluded the first part of this work with a brief discussion of the diction of argument because it is in the domain of argumentation, the domain where the assessment of reasons is central, that warrant constructions find their chief employment, providing a rich and subtle basis for the formulation of reasoned discourse.

Part Two

INTRODUCTION

IN the next three chapters I shall extend warrant statement analysis into the region of evaluative discourse. Broadly speaking, the approach involves a merging of a prescriptivism of the sort developed by R. M. Hare with the warrant statement analysis developed in the first part of this work. Specifically, I shall argue that value judgments can be viewed as warrant statements that have imperatives for material components.

In contrast to Part One, I shall here examine certain philosophical texts in detail. Chapter VI will begin with a careful investigation of Moore's discussion of the meaning of the term 'good'. I shall argue that his position involves four cardinal points, and that a sequence of succeeding theories concerning the meaning of evaluative discourse can be viewed as variations upon Moore's four-part theory (hence the title of Chapter VI: Variations on a Four-Part Theme). The central thesis of Chapter VI is this: Moore's position contains a grave error that his successors (and would-be critics) share with him, and it is this error that is the source of many perplexities that have stymied contemporary ethical theorizing.

These last few remarks should explain the seemingly disproportionate space allocated to a detailed examination of the writings of G. E. Moore. To understand the current controversies in ethical theory, one must understand Moore, and furthermore, in order to settle these controversies, it is necessary to reveal the errors in the way Moore posed problems for twentieth-century thought.

VI

VARIATIONS ON A FOUR-PART THEME[1]

FOR G. E. Moore, ethics is concerned with a 'certain predicate "good" and its converse "bad"',[2] and the questions concerning this predicate—and hence the questions of ethics itself—can be divided into three classes:

(1) 'What is *meant* by good?'
(2) 'What things are good in themselves?'
(3) 'By what means will we be able to make what exists in the world as good as possible?'[3]

Of the three questions, Moore considers the first theoretically most important, but he also stresses the importance of answering the second question; he describes such answers as defining *the* good and contrasts this with defining good itself. This contrast lies at the heart of the naturalistic fallacy as Moore uses the notion, and the fallacy cannot be understood unless it is kept in mind. In point of fact, the phrase 'naturalistic fallacy' is generally given a

---

[1] Since the subject of this chapter is largely historical, I shall make but few references to warrant statements. In Chapter VII warrant statement analysis will be used in an effort to cope with the problems exposed in this chapter.

[2] G. E. Moore, *Principia Ethica*, Cambridge University Press (Cambridge, 1903), p. 1.

[3] These three questions are listed in a summary passage at the beginning of Chapter II of *Principia Ethica*.

significance entirely different from that originally assigned to it by Moore. Since I propose to use this notion in its original sense, I shall take somewhat elaborate measures to show what Moore meant by it. I shall return to the naturalistic fallacy later (in § 3); first, let me say something about Moore's discussion of what is meant by good.

Moore insists that his search for the meaning of good is not a verbal matter.

> My business is solely with that object or idea which I hold rightly or wrongly, that the word is generally used to stand for. What I want to discover is the nature of that object or idea, and about this I am extremely anxious to arrive at agreement.[1]

Concerning this object or idea, he is looking for a definition that 'states what are the parts which invariably compose a certain whole'.[2] Thus Moore's original question, 'What is meant by good?' is transformed into the more specific question, 'What are the parts which invariably compose that object or idea that the term "good" is generally used to stand for?'

Moore will argue that no such definition is possible because good is a simple notion, but before going into this let me pause here to note two important assumptions that Moore makes at the very outset of his investigation. Moore certainly believes that the term 'good' *stands for* something, be it an object or an idea. In *Principia Ethica* he never defended this basic assumption, and later, even in the face of an explicit challenge from C. D. Broad, he evaded the issue with the following reply:

> He himself [Broad] however, has chosen not to discuss this particular question, and I do not think that any of the other contributors have discussed it either. I do not therefore propose to discuss it myself.[3]

This assumption that the term 'good' stands for something can be derived from two further assumptions that Moore plainly makes:

(1) Value judgments are assertions.

[1] Moore, p. 6.   [2] Ibid., p. 9.
[3] P. A. Schilp, editor, *The Philosophy of G. E. Moore*, Northwestern University (Chicago, 1942), p. 536.

(2) If value judgments are assertions, they ascribe a property to the thing evaluated.[1]

These two assumptions exert a powerful influence on Moore's thinking, indeed, it takes only one further doctrine to supply the logical foundation for the main lines of his entire theory.

2. THE ARGUMENT FROM SIMPLICITY

In the previous section we saw how Moore interprets the question, 'How is good to be defined?' He answers it in the following way:

> But if we understand the question in this sense, my answer to it may seem a very disappointing one. If I am asked, 'What is good?' my answer is that good is good, and that is the end of the matter. Or if I am asked 'How is good to be defined?' my answer is that it cannot be defined, and that is all I have to say about it.[2]

Expanding on this claim he states:

> My point is that 'good' is a simple notion, just as yellow is a simple notion; that, just as you cannot, by any manner or means explain to any one who does not know it, what yellow is, so you cannot explain what good is. Definitions of the kind that I am asking for, definitions which describe the real nature of the object or notion denoted by a word, and which do not merely tell us what the word is used to mean, are only possible when the object or notion in question is something complex.[3]

These two passages invoke a constellation of questions, and for more than fifty years Moore's critics have busied themselves over them. But rather than take issue with these claims individually, I shall deal with them in a more radical way: I shall argue that the entire discussion exhibits the fallacy of *ignoratio elenchi*, for even if the claim for simplicity and hence indefinability is accepted, the important conclusions that Moore wishes to draw from them simply do not follow.

[1] The two assumptions can be combined as 'Since value judgments are assertions, they ascribe a property to the thing evaluated.' But as we shall see in Chapter VII, it is important to keep these two assumptions separate, for there is an important sense in which we can accept the first and yet reject the second.

[2] Moore, p. 7.

[3] Ibid., p. 7.

The Argument from Simplicity

What basic theses does Moore wish to establish with the help of the argument from simplicity? They become clear if we examine the continuation of the first passage cited above.

> But disappointing as these answers may appear, they are of the very last importance. To readers who are familiar with philosophic terminology, I can express their importance by saying that they amount to this: That propositions about the good are all of them synthetic and never analytic; and that is plainly no trivial matter. And the same thing may be expressed more popularly by saying that, if I am right, then nobody can foist upon us such an axiom as that 'Pleasure is the only good' or that 'The good is the desired' on the pretense that this is 'the meaning of the word'.[1]

These conclusions surely are—to use Moore's phrase—'of the very last importance', and furthermore, given suitable clarification, I would be willing to accept them as correct. But do they follow, as Moore thinks they do, from the claim that good is a simple notion? The answer is, no. To show this, let us concede Moore's dubious premises and see if these conclusions follow from them. In the first place we shall allow that the term 'good' stands for some object or idea. Furthermore, we shall not take issue with the claim that this object or idea is simple, that is to say, not composed of parts (whatever this may mean). Does it then follow that propositions about the good are all of them synthetic, never analytic? A counter-example will show that it does not.

Consider the hedonist who is convinced that pleasure and goodness are the same characteristic. For him the statement 'Pleasure is good' is analytic and its truth follows from the very meaning of the terms employed. Moore's argument would have no bearing upon this claim, for the hedonist could acknowledge that Moore is correct in calling good a simple notion, and then argue that pleasure is also a simple notion, in fact, the *same* simple notion that is designated by the term 'good'. This shows clearly that the statement, 'propositions about the good are all of them synthetic and never analytic', in no way follows from the argument from simplicity.

This same point can be made in another way. If we accept Moore's argument at face value, it would have the following curious result. It would have absolutely no bearing upon any naturalistic theory that identifies goodness with a simple notion;

[1] Moore, p. 7.

it would, however, refute A. C. Ewing's intuitionist theory which treats good as a *complex* non-natural property. Moore could hardly accept this result.

Though the above argument is uncomplicated it is not unimportant. It establishes beyond doubt that Moore's entire discussion of the simplicity of good has absolutely no bearing upon the basic theses he is trying to establish. But if it is possible to dismiss Moore's central claim with such ease, how can the genuine influence of his work in ethics be explained? The answer, let me suggest, is this: though the entire argument from simplicity is misguided, entangled in it are two other arguments of great moment. The first is the argument against the so-called *naturalistic fallacy*. As we shall see, it is a simple argument, and though sound, ultimately is of slight systematic importance. The second argument has come to be known as the *open question argument*. It should not be treated lightly, for if it is sound, as I think it is, Moore can use it to make good his claim that naturalistic theories (*as he understands them*) are all of them fundamentally mistaken.

Unfortunately, the argument from simplicity continually stands in the way of a clear comprehension of Moore's important insights, for it reasserts itself throughout the development of his position. Hence, in order to grasp Moore's position, an entire reconstruction of his argument is necessary. The purpose of this reconstruction is to exhibit the naturalistic fallacy and the open question argument free of the confusions introduced by the misguided argument from simplicity.

Will this reconstruction faithfully represent Moore's thought? I am afraid not. But it is not my intention to represent Moore's position in a way faithful to his own thinking, for his own thinking about his position was confused. My purpose is to present Moore's position in a clear and unambiguous form. That Moore held to something like the position presented can be adequately documented from the text; that he explicitly thought of his position in the way I present it is obviously not the case.

3. THE NATURALISTIC FALLACY

A proper understanding of what Moore means by the naturalistic fallacy is not difficult if we pay close attention to the context in which it is introduced. The naturalistic fallacy makes its debut in

Section Ten immediately following Moore's discussion of the distinction between definitions of good and definitions of *the* good. Let me cite this crucial, yet often ignored, passage at length:

> I do not mean to say that *the* good, that which is good, is thus indefinable; if I did think so, I should not be writing on Ethics, for my main object is to help towards discovering that definition. It is just because I think there will be less risk or error in our search for a definition of 'the good' that I am now insisting that *good* is indefinable. I must try to explain the difference between these two. I suppose that it may be granted that good is an adjective. Well, 'the good', that which is good, must therefore be the substantive to which the adjective 'good' will apply: it must be the whole of that to which the adjective will apply, and must *always* truly apply to it. But if it is that to which the adjective will apply, it must be something different from that adjective itself; and the whole of that something different, whatever it is, will be our definition of *the* good. Now it may be that this something will have other adjectives, beside 'good' that will apply to it. It may be full of pleasure, for example; it may be intelligent: and if these two adjectives are really part of its definition then it will certainly be true, that pleasure and intelligence are good. And many people appear to think that, if we say 'Pleasure and intelligence are good', or if we say 'Only pleasure and intelligence are good', we are defining 'good'. Well, I cannot deny that propositions of this nature may sometimes be called definitions; I do not know well enough how the word is generally used to decide upon this point. I only wish it to be understood that that is not what I mean when I say there is no possible definition of good, and that I shall not mean this if I use the word again. I do most fully believe that some true proposition of the form 'Intelligence is good and intelligence alone is good' can be found; if none could be found, our definition of *the* good would be impossible. As it is, I believe *the* good to be definable; and yet I still say that good itself is indefinable.[1]

As Moore's argument continues, he needlessly returns to the notion of simplicity, but a remark he makes in this context leads directly to the notion of the naturalistic fallacy. He starts by saying that there is nothing peculiar in the conception of a simple property. As an example of such a property he suggests the colour

[1] Moore, pp. 8–9.

yellow. An attempt might be made to define yellow in terms of certain light vibrations, but as Moore points out: 'a moment's reflection is sufficient to show that those light vibrations are not themselves what we mean by yellow'.[1] From the mere fact, Moore is saying, that they are invariably correlated we cannot infer that they are the same thing. It is precisely this fallacy, no other, that is involved in the naturalistic fallacy concerning good. This becomes abundantly clear if we follow Moore's elaboration upon this example in the paragraph following it.

> Yet a mistake of this simple kind has commonly been made about 'good'. It may be true that all things which are good are also something else, just as it is true that all things which are yellow produce a certain kind of vibration in the light. And it is a fact, that Ethics aims at discovering what are these other properties belonging to all things which are good. But far too many philosophers have thought that when they named those other properties they were actually defining good: that these properties, in fact, were simply not 'other', but absolutely and entirely the same with goodness. This view I propose to call the 'naturalistic fallacy' and of it I shall now endeavour to dispose.[2]

Here the statement of the naturalistic fallacy is entirely unambiguous, and may be explained by Moore's distinction between definitions of *the* good and definitions of good itself. A definition of *the* good takes the following form:

X is good if, and only if, x is ϕ.

Here ϕ is a property distinct from good. Moore has no theoretical objections to definitions of this kind, but points out that it is a fallacy—he calls it the naturalistic fallacy—to confuse this kind of definition with a definition of goodness itself. The implicit inference which produces this confusion is of the following form:

X is good if, and only if, x is ϕ; therefore, good and ϕ are identical.

To use the language of logicians, the naturalistic fallacy is the illicit inference from extensional equivalence to intensional equivalence.

That this is the correct interpretation of the naturalistic fallacy

[1] Moore, p. 10.   [2] Ibid., p. 10.

is borne out by further examination of the text. In Section Twelve Moore offers two more examples of this fallacious inference:

> . . . when I say 'I am pleased', I do not mean that 'I' am the same thing as 'having pleasure'. And similarly no difficulty need be found in saying that 'pleasure is good' and yet not mean that 'pleasure' is the same thing as 'good', that pleasure *means* good, that good means pleasure.[1]

> When we say that an orange is yellow, we do not think our statement binds us to hold that 'orange' means nothing else than 'yellow' . . .[2]

These two examples bear out the interpretation of the fallacy I have given.

A great deal of confusion is avoided when we recognize that the naturalistic fallacy stands quite on its own; it is not logically dependent upon either of the further claims that good is a *simple* or a *non-natural* property. This independence from the doctrine of non-natural properties is explicitly stated by Moore in the following passage:

> Even if it [good] were a natural object, that would not alter the nature of the fallacy nor diminish its importance one whit. All that I have said would remain quite equally true: only the name I have called it would not be so appropriate as I think it is.[3]

Though Moore does not seem to recognize this, it should be equally clear that the naturalistic fallacy is independent of the claim that good is a simple notion. To paraphrase the above passage, even if good were a *complex* object, that would not alter the nature of the fallacy nor diminish its importance one whit. The inference from extensional equivalence to intensional equivalence is fallacious whether the notions involved are simple or complex.

Thus having extracted an unambiguous formulation of the naturalistic fallacy from the text, two questions are in order. (1) Is it a genuine fallacy? (2) Can it be shown that the position known as ethical naturalism can be refuted on the grounds that all those who hold this position *must* be guilty of committing this fallacy?

(1) There is no need to dwell at length on the first question. It should be obvious that the pattern of reasoning Moore calls 'the naturalistic fallacy' is genuinely fallacious. There is surely no

---

[1] Moore, p. 13.   [2] Ibid., p. 13.   [3] Ibid., p. 14.

warrant for inferring intensional equivalence from extensional equivalence or for using the sufficient conditions for extensional equivalence as the sufficient conditions for intensional equivalence. To speak less technically, because two properties are invariably associated, we cannot infer their identity. No one will take issue with this claim.

(2) The second question, concerning the relationship between the naturalistic fallacy and ethical naturalism, is more complicated, for it depends for its answer upon a proper understanding of the position known as ethical naturalism. When Moore speaks of a *naturalistic* theory he is thinking of a theory containing the following claim: the term 'good' is the name of some natural property, and hence, value judgments function to indicate that things possess this property. In Moore's sense of the word, a naturalist in ethics would assert that a value judgment is merely one sort of factual judgment. Such a definition of ethical naturalism is probably too narrow, but this is the sense in which Moore uses the label, and until further notice I shall use it in this way as well.

Now Moore is particularly anxious to refute ethical naturalism, so our second question takes the following form: can Moore use his conception of the naturalistic fallacy to show that 'good' is *not* the name of a natural property? The answer to this question is plainly no, and this answer is based upon a simple point of logic. Thus far Moore can only assert the following hypothetical conclusion: If a hedonist (for example) argues in the following way, 'A thing is good if, and only if, it is pleasant; therefore, goodness and pleasantness are identical,' then this hedonist is arguing fallaciously. But showing that a pattern of reasoning is fallacious does not show that a conclusion based upon it is false. The most that Moore has done is to close a seductive road to naturalism, but the general refutation of ethical naturalism is still to be brought forward. This will be found, I believe, in an argument quite distinct from that concerning the naturalistic fallacy, an argument that has come to be known as the Open Question Argument.

4. THE OPEN QUESTION ARGUMENT

Confronted with the naturalistic fallacy, the naturalist can respond with a strong counter-argument. The naturalist, according to Moore, identifies goodness with some natural property simply because they are invariably associated. The staunch naturalist will not admit this, but reply that when he thinks of things that are good, he can recognize only one notion which he indifferently calls by the name 'good' and 'pleasant'.

Moore anticipates this rejoinder and answers it explicitly, and in his reply we come to the Open Question Argument:

> . . . whoever will attentively consider with himself what is actually before his mind when he asks the question 'Is pleasure (or whatever it may be) after all good?' he can easily satisfy himself that he is not merely wondering whether pleasure is pleasant. And if he will try this experiment with each suggested definition in succession, he may become expert enough to recognize that in every case he has before his mind a unique object, about which a distinct question may be asked. Everyone does in fact understand the question 'Is this good?' When he thinks of it, his state of mind is different from what it would be, were he asked 'Is this pleasant, or desired, or approved.' [1]

At first glance the argument seems to involve nothing more than a direct appeal to introspective data. In order to discover something, the reader is asked to 'attentively consider with himself what is actually before his mind'. Now if Moore's argument simply came to this—introspectively we can note a categorical difference between goodness and any given natural property—there would be very little that could be said either for or against his position. We would be left with the unsatisfactory procedure of polling those philosophers whose credentials are in order and then declaring Moore the loser. But Moore does not *simply* ask us to contemplate items before our mind, instead, he asks us to reflect upon the question 'Is pleasure (or whatever it may be) after all good?' and then he tells us that we can easily satisfy ourselves that we are 'not merely wondering whether pleasure is pleasant'. These instructions can be followed without giving the inquiry an introspective cast, and as a matter of fact, many philosophers who would reject appeals to introspective data have found Moore's claim totally convincing.

Exactly what is the point of posing such a question? The underpinning of the argument seems to be this: if 'pleasant' and 'good' were simply alternative names for the same thing, then anyone

[1] Moore, pp. 16–17.

who knew the meaning of these two terms would thereby recognize that the question 'Is pleasure after all good?' is as empty
as the question 'Is pleasure after all pleasant?' Moore claims that
the first question is not like the second in this respect, and even
beyond this he suggests that, by trying this experiment on a
sequence of definitions, we can become expert enough to see that
no factual predicate will trivialize the question in the required
way. Pleasure isn't simply the wrong *thing* to identify with goodness, it is the wrong *kind* of thing.[1]

Thus Moore seems to have in mind two different kinds of predicates that he has recognized in paradigm cases: following the
tradition we can call one category *descriptive*, the other category
evaluative. In the open question argument he attempts to *exhibit*
this difference by juxtaposing these two kinds of predicates within
a specially constructed question. It is important to realize that the
open question argument yields no account of this difference, and
for that reason does not supply a sure guide when we enter the
twilight zone between evaluative and descriptive discourse. If I
describe the governor as a conscientious administrator, have I
described him or have I evaluated him? In other words, is this
statement more like the paradigm 'He is a good governor' or the
paradigm 'He is a short governor'? The answer, of course, is that
it is like the first statement in some ways and like the second statement in other ways, and as matters stand we are not in a position
to articulate these similarities and differences. Thus the terms
'evaluative' and 'descriptive' are not names for antecedently
understood categories; they mark out areas for investigation.

But even if the open question argument does not explain the
difference between evaluative and descriptive discourse, it does
draw our attention to a difference, at least for paradigm cases. I
think that anyone who has followed Moore's argument will admit
the plausibility of this claim. He may, however, hesitate to accept
it, anticipating a wide range of unfortunate results. Within the
context of Moore's theory it leads to the doctrine of those ghostly
entities, non-natural properties; while in the hands of the logical

[1] This style of reasoning has been undercut by the recognition of referential
opacity: we can know the same thing under two different names or under two different descriptions and still not know that these names or descriptions refer to the same
thing. But we can, I think, safely ignore referential opacity, since it doesn't seem to
raise difficulties in the present context.

positivists (e.g. A. J. Ayer) it leads to a most unholy scepticism. By anticipating these dire results a critic can invoke a kind of *reductio ad absurdum* against the open question argument and then, in spite of its obvious plausibility, reject it. In the next chapter I shall show how the force of the open question argument can be incorporated (and understood) within a satisfactory treatment of evaluative discourse, but before doing this, I shall show how it can be used in the derivation of unsatisfactory results.

5. VARIATION I, MOORE'S INTUITIONISM

In § 1 of this chapter we saw that Moore made the two following assumptions:

(1) Value judgments are assertions.
(2) If value judgments are assertions, they ascribe a property to the thing evaluated.

To these two assumptions we need only add the result of the open question argument—that value judgments are not factual judgments—and we can derive the main lines of Moore's intuitionism. The derivation of non-natural properties is all too obvious. Since value judgments are assertions, they ascribe properties (from 1 and 2), but since they are not factual judgments, they do not ascribe natural properties (from the open question argument). Hence, value judgments ascribe some kind of non-natural property. Moore's intuitionism follows as the natural epistemology for coping with these non-natural properties.

I shall now represent Moore's system by the following four-part schema:

Instuitionism

(1) Value judgments are assertions.
(2) If value judgments are assertions they ascribe a property to the thing evaluated.
(3) Value judgments are not a kind of factual judgment.

⎫
⎬ entail
⎭

(4) Value judgments ascribe a non-natural property to the thing evaluated.

Moore plainly accepts the premises on the left, and since they entail the conclusion on the right, we can view his espousal of the doctrine of non-natural properties as the result of reasoning, not the result of a private intuitive insight that few philosophers have duplicated.

I propose to treat the doctrine of non-natural properties as the *reductio ad absurdem* of Moore's position. In the end, the existence of non-natural properties can be settled only by an appeal to inspection, and since with time the consensus of expert opinion has run overwhelmingly against Moore, it would seem that his position is no longer a live option. But if we are to reject the doctrine of non-natural properties, then we must also reject at least one of the three doctrines that entail it. Historically this way of thinking led directly into non-cognitivism, as I shall now show.

6. VARIATION II, NON-COGNITIVISM

Leibniz criticized the Cartesians on the grounds that their principles led directly to the heretical doctrines of Spinoza. With about equal justice, Moore can be held responsible for the emergence of non-cognitivism in contemporary ethical theory. To show this, I shall first represent the transition from intuitionism to non-cognitivism schematically, and then, secondly, show that the thought of A. J. Ayer (the archetypal non-cognitivist in ethics) moved along just the lines indicated.

The derivation of non-cognitivism begins with a denial of the doctrine of non-natural properties, and then by an elementary law of logic at least one of the three propositions that conjointly entail it must be denied. With this in mind, the road to non-cognitivism is a straight one. To begin with, the open question argument in one of its forms is explicitly accepted. Next, the assumption that if value judgments are assertions they ascribe properties is also accepted.[1] Having thus accepted two planks of Moore's platform, the doctrine that value judgments are assertions must now be rejected. In rejecting the claim that value judgments are assertions, non-cognitivism is embraced; indeed, this is all I mean by calling a theory non-cognitivist.

---

[1] I don't think that the non-cognitivists realize that they make this assumption, but without it, they have no right to draw the conclusions they do.

Non-cognitivism becomes the second variation upon a four-part theme, and can be represented as follows:[1]

Non-cognitivism

(2) If value judgments are assertions they ascribe a property to the thing evaluated.

(3) Value judgments are not a kind of factual judgment.

(4') Value judgments do not ascribe a non-natural property to the thing evaluated.

entail

(1') Value judgments are not assertions.

That the three propositions on the left directly entail the conclusion on the right can be seen from the following brief argument:

If value judgments are assertions, they ascribe a property to the thing evaluated.	(2)
Such a property must be either natural or non-natural.	(taut.)
It cannot be a natural property.	(3)
It cannot be a non-natural property.	(4')
∴ Value judgments are not assertions.	

Just this line of reasoning is followed in the sixth chapter of A. J. Ayer's *Language, Truth and Logic*, where we find a simple and elegant statement of non-cognitivism.[2] The starting-point for Ayer's theory is the acceptance of Moore's critique of naturalism. For systematic reasons which we need not discuss (they concern the defence of the verifiability principle), he wishes to deny that 'statements of ethical value can be translated into statements of empirical fact'.[3] Ayer's argument in favour of this point is merely a restatement of Moore's open question argument:

. . . since it is not self-contradictory to say that some pleasant things are not good, or that some bad things are desired, it

---

[1] I have taken the numbering for Moore's position as canonical, and have affixed a prime to indicate the denial of one of Moore's principles.

[2] Though other statements of non-cognitivism are stronger on the constructive side, none improves upon Ayer's reasons for denying that value judgments are assertions.

[3] A. J. Ayer, *Language, Truth and Logic* (London, 1947), p. 104.

cannot be the case that the sentence '*x* is good' is equivalent to '*x* is pleasant' or '*x* is desired'.[1]

The only change here is that Ayer talks about the negative proposition 'Pleasant things are not good' as not being self-contradictory where Moore spoke of the affirmative proposition 'Pleasant things are good' as not being analytic. The two ways of speaking are, of course, equivalent. Ayer cites but few naturalistic theories; he, like Moore, is confident that this pattern of argument will refute them all. No matter what empirical property we assign to a thing, it will never be contradictory to say that an object possesses that property but is not good.

With naturalism out of the way, Ayer turns next upon intuitionism:

> In admitting that normative ethical concepts are irreducible to empirical concepts, we seem to be leaving the way clear for the 'absolutist's' view of ethics—that is, the view that statements of value are not controlled by observation, as ordinary empirical propositions are, but only by a mysterious 'intellectual intuitionism'.[2]

Ayer closes the road to intuitionism by invoking the verifiability principle, and though the verifiability principle is now largely in disrepute, I shall not cavil over its use, since in substance I here agree with Ayer: the doctrine of non-natural properties with its attendant intuitionism must be rejected.

Having rejected both naturalism and intuitionism, Ayer moves directly to one of his central theses:

> The presence of an ethical symbol in a proposition adds nothing to its factual content.[3]

Certain value judgments, Ayer would admit, do have cognitive content. When we say, 'You acted wrongly in stealing that money,' we are asserting that you stole money, but the additional claim that the act was wrong adds nothing, according to Ayer, to the cognitive content of the sentence. Thus the sentence, 'Stealing is wrong,' does not express a genuine proposition at all; it puts forward no claim that can be properly considered true or false. Thus Ayer does not claim that value judgments never express truth claims, but he does maintain that a value judgment as such

[1] A. J. Ayer, p. 105.   [2] Ibid., p. 106.   [3] Ibid., p. 107.

does not put forward a truth claim; hence we are right in calling him a non-cognitivist.

Let us examine the structure of Ayer's argument. He has made two initial claims (which, by the way, I find unobjectionable):

(1) Value judgments are not like such statements as 'This is pleasant', 'This is approved', or 'This is desired'. To use Moore's terminology, value judgments do not ascribe natural properties to things.

(2) Value judgments do not ascribe some intuitively grasped non-natural properties to things.

From these two propositions Ayer immediately moves to his non-cognitivist thesis:

(3) Value judgments, as such, are not genuine assertions.

Since it should be clear that these two initial statements do not entail the third statement, Ayer is either guilty of a logical blunder or he has employed some suppressed premiss that, for one reason or another, he has not made explicit.

If we return to the text we can find such a suppressed premiss at work. When Ayer employs the open question argument he proceeds in the manner of G. E. Moore, testing only statements that involve an empirical predication. Now it might be the case that certain synthetic statements do not have the form of the statements that Ayer has examined, hence all that Ayer has established is that value judgments are unlike one sort of synthetic statement. But Ayer does not explore the possibility that there could be another class of synthetic statements that value judgments do resemble closely. *This does not even occur to him*, and from this fact I think we are warranted in asserting that Ayer assumes that, to be assertions, value judgments would have to function to ascribe properties.

There are really two options—either grant that Ayer makes this assumption or declare that his argument is invalid at a trivial level. Since the text supports the more charitable interpretation, I shall say that Ayer makes this assumption, and hence conclude that the pattern for non-cognitivism accurately represents the logic of his position.

But in all this, no mention has been made of Ayer's emotivism.

The reason for this is that emotivism is just one way in which non-cognitivism can be developed in the direction of a positive account of the nature of value judgments. Once the decision is made that value judgments are not assertions, the door is left open to any number of accounts of what they are instead. Ayer suggests that they are used 'to express feeling about certain objects' or perhaps 'to arouse feeling, and so stimulate action'.[1] But those who maintain that value judgments neither express nor arouse emotion can still remain within the non-cognitivist camp. R. M. Hare, who maintains that value judgments are a special brand of prescriptive discourse, is, it seems to me, a non-cognitivist, but he repudiates Ayer's account of value judgments guiding conduct through arousing emotion.

If we recognize that emotivism is only one form (and probably the weakest form) that non-cognitivism can take, we will not make the mistake of trying to refute the entire position by presenting arguments that apply to but one of its forms. If non-cognitivism is to be refuted, its defining characteristic must be attacked; this is the claim that value judgments, whatever they might be, are not genuine assertions. I shall now argue that this central claim is mistaken.

In the first place, it is important to note that the pattern of argument for non-cognitivism contains one vital weakness. In following Ayer's discussion we get the impression that the open question argument combined with the denial of non-natural properties leads directly to the claim that value judgments (as such) are not assertions. We now see that this is not so. In order for this conclusion to be derived, the further assumption must be made that if value judgments are assertions they then ascribe properties.[2] And this all-important assumption is nowhere defended; it is not even explicitly recognized. Hence, we have a right to assert that Ayer has not established the non-cognitivist conclusion, nor, to be dogmatic, do I think has anyone else.

Furthermore, I would like to suggest that a philosopher would accept the non-cognitivist thesis only under the influence of seemingly overwhelming theoretical reasons, for the doctrine is

---

[1] A. J. Ayer, p. 107.

[2] Perhaps Ayer employs some other assumption as the requisite suppressed premiss, but in any case, this will not affect the remarks that are made in this paragraph, for the charge will still stand that he has not established his case.

incredible on the very face of it. As Ayer develops his position it seems that Moore's intuitionism is the only alternative to non-cognitivism, and to a tough-minded empiricist, this is no alternative at all. But we see now that we are not forced to choose between intuitionism and non-cognitivism; if the analysis thus far is correct, we can escape between the horns of this dilemma by denying a doctrine common to both intuitionism and non-cognitivism, the doctrine that if value judgments are assertions they must ascribe a property to the thing evaluated.

If a positive argument is needed to establish the claim that value judgments are assertions, the five following points would seem to do the job. Like most assertions, value judgments: (1) are expressed in the indicative mode; (2) are normally called true or false; (3) admit of tenses;[1] (4) are believed; and (5) give rise to expectations whose fulfilment or non-fulfilment will have a bearing upon our future expectations. Perhaps no one of these points is sufficient in itself, but taken together they constitute an overwhelming case in favour of the claim that value judgments are assertions. I shall thus consider the claim that value judgments are not assertions as the *reductio ad absurdum* of that pattern of reasoning I have called non-cognitivism.

7. VARIATION III, NATURALISM

The road back to naturalism can begin with a critique of the weak points of intuitionism and non-cognitivism. Ayer was right in denying the doctrine of non-natural properties, but wrong in declaring that value judgments are not assertions. Moore, on the other hand, was wrong in maintaining the doctrine of non-natural properties, but right in declaring that value judgments are assertions. Therefore, since value judgments are assertions and do not function to ascribe non-natural properties, they must function to ascribe natural properties.

This seems compelling until we notice that the dual claim that value judgments are assertions and do not ascribe non-natural properties does not entail the claim that they ascribe natural properties. This argument is grounded on the further assumption

---

[1] This fact is particularly embarrassing for anyone who wishes to account for value judgments using imperatives as a model.

that has played a key role in the two positions already examined; this, of course, is the assumption that if value judgments are assertions they must ascribe some property to the thing evaluated. Hence, naturalism becomes the third variation upon the four-part theme:

Naturalism

(1) Value judgments are assertions.
(2) If value judgments are assertions they ascribe a property to the thing evaluated.
(4') Value judgments do not ascribe a non-natural property to the thing evaluated.

$\left.\vphantom{\begin{array}{c}1\\2\\3\\4\end{array}}\right\}$ entail

(3') Value judgments are a kind of factual judgment.

But in accepting the force of Moore's open question argument, we have already denied that value judgments are a kind of factual judgment; hence, this position must be rejected along with the previous two.[1]

8. CONCLUDING REMARKS

Let us now bring together the three positions we have examined in this chapter:

Intuitionism

(1) Value judgments are assertions.
(2) If value judgments are assertions they ascribe a property to the thing evaluated.
(3) Value judgments are not a kind of factual judgment.

$\left.\vphantom{\begin{array}{c}1\\2\\3\\4\end{array}}\right\}$ entail

(4) Value judgments ascribe a non-natural property to the thing evaluated.

---

[1] I have not chosen to examine the writings of an actual naturalist such as Ralph Barton Perry or John Dewey since in their writings they rarely hit these matters head on. I shall return to ethical naturalism—and defend a version of it—in the concluding chapter.

Non-cognitivism

(2) If value judgments are assertions they ascribe a property to the thing evaluated.

(3) Value judgments are not a kind of factual judgment.

(4′) Value judgments do not ascribe a non-natural property to the thing evaluated.

} entail (1′) Value judgments are not assertions.

Naturalism

(1) Value judgments are assertions.

(2) If value judgments are assertions they ascribe a property to the thing evaluated.

(4′) Value judgments do not ascribe a non-natural property to the thing evaluated.

} entail (3′) Value judgments are a kind of factual judgment.

Taken together, these three patterns exhibit a certain mathematical elegance. Throughout, one assumption is held constant:

(2) If value judgments are assertions, they ascribe a property to the thing evaluated.

Then to this assumption two of the three following doctrines are added:

(1) Value judgments are assertions.

(3) Value judgments are not a kind of factual judgment.

(4′) Value judgments do not ascribe a non-natural property to the thing evaluated.

In fact, the three patterns exhaust all of the combinations of these three doctrines taken two at a time. But the most interesting feature is this: if we combine any two of these doctrines with assumption (2), the three doctrines taken together entail the denial of the remaining doctrine in the list.

These results, I would argue, are more than mere mathematical curiosities. In the course of this discussion I have accepted doctrines (1), (3), and (4′) as *prima facie* truths, and thus have rejected out of hand any theory that leads to the denial of any one of them. But if the second doctrine is maintained as a suppressed and unrecognized premiss, then assertions (1), (3), and (4′) will appear incompatible, and thus it will appear impossible to construct a consistent theory that can accommodate all three. I suggest that the apparent irreconcilability of these three doctrines has been a major cause of the impasse in the recent studies of the nature of evaluative discourse.

This brings us to the final variation upon this four-part theme. If we wish to accept propositions (1), (3), and (4′), we must reject proposition (2). This yields the final schema which, for want of a better title, I have called Pattern *W*.

Variation IV, Pattern W

(1) Value judgments are assertions.

(3) Value judgments are not a kind of factual judgment.

(4′) Value judgments do not ascribe a non-natural property to the thing evaluated.

entail

(2′) Although value judgments are assertions, they do not ascribe a property to the thing evaluated.

Pattern *W* yields only a negative result; it tells us what value judgments are not. The job of constructing a positive account of the logical character of value judgments is the task of Chapter VII.

VII

VALUE JUDGMENTS AS
WARRANT STATEMENTS

THE conclusion of Chapter VI was that value judgments, although they are assertions, do not ascribe a property to the thing evaluated. This conclusion would carry more force if it were supplemented with a clear explication of the notion of ascribing a property, but let me confess at once that I am unable to offer such a clear explication. As a way of avoiding a great many technical problems that I am unable to cope with, I shall simply say that we are ascribing a property to a thing whenever we *say something about it*. This is all that I shall say, and I do not propose to elaborate further upon it. If I am asked (for example) *what* property is ascribed to Perry in the sentence 'Perry discovered the North Pole', I shall take my cue from certain logicians and say it is precisely the property that is ascribed to Perry in the sentence 'Perry discovered the North Pole'. This does not answer any significant questions about the status of properties, but it does provide a convenient way of avoiding questions that I have chosen not to discuss.

But if we adopt this very generous definition of ascribing properties, it turns out that value judgments do, after all, ascribe properties to the thing evaluated. If I say that Job was a good man, I have certainly *said something about* Job, and this, on the convention just introduced, is sufficient grounds for saying that we have ascribed a property to him. In order to bring the conclusion of the preceding chapter into line with this new convention, I propose to draw a distinction between two kinds of properties: *material properties* and *warrant properties*. To ascribe a material property to a thing is to say something about it by way of offering a direct description; to assign a warrant property to a thing is to say something about it, but only indirectly, by saying something about the status of the grounds on behalf of some expression concerning it. Thus, if the analysis in Chapter II is correct, the remark 'It is highly probable that there is life on Mars' ascribes a warrant property to life on Mars, while the statement 'A green band appears in the equatorial region of Mars during the summer months' ascribes a material property to a region of Mars.

If we reflect upon the discussion of Chapter VI, it should be clear that throughout we were thinking of ascribing properties in a material sense only. Thus, a more accurate statement of Pattern *W* takes the following form:[1]

Pattern W

(1) Value judgments are assertions. (3) Value judgments are not a kind of factual judgment. (4') Value judgments do not ascribe a *material* non-natural property to the thing evaluated.	entail	(2') Although value judgments are assertions, they do not ascribe a *material* property to the thing evaluated.

Notice that (2') is *not* equivalent to the claim that value judgments ascribe a warrant property to the thing evaluated. This would follow only if every property is either a material property or a warrant property. No such claim has been made, and, in point of fact, it probably isn't true. Thus, Pattern *W* supplies no easy proof of the warrant character of value judgments.

[1] The other three patterns should be amended along similar lines.

2. THE PRESCRIPTIVE FORCE OF VALUE JUDGMENTS[1]

This playing with logical possibilities, this 'unearthly ballet of bloodless categories' must come to an end if we are to make further progress towards a proper understanding of evaluative discourse. We must cease examining theories about value judgments and study the object directly.

Wittgenstein has suggested that we compare words with tools, and just as we can come to understand the nature of a tool by seeing how it is used, so too we should search for the meaning of terms by finding the uses to which they are put.

> 43. For a *large* class of cases—though not for all—in which we employ the word 'meaning' it can be defined thus: the meaning of a word is its use in the language.[2]

But if we turn to the uses of evaluative terms in ordinary discourse, we are immediately confronted with an embarrassment of riches; value judgments have a seemingly endless number of uses. Here are a few of these uses presented in no particular order: (1) they are used to praise; (2) they are used to advise; (3) they are used to rank things; (4) they are used to condemn things; (5) they are used in greetings; (6) they are used in uttering threats; (7) they are used to express emotion; (8) they are used in grading; (9) they are used in insults; and so on. Thus, if we accept the doctrine that the meaning of a term is its use in the language, we seem forced to say that value judgments have a seemingly unending number of meanings.

But the analogy between words and tools need not lead to this radical pluralism. As Wittgenstein realized, the same tool can be used to perform a variety of jobs; a hammer can be used for driving in nails or for banging them out from the other side, for tapping things into place or smashing them apart. The uses of a hammer are probably as varied as the uses of value judgments,

---

[1] The reader familiar with the literature will recognize that a great deal of this discussion concerning the prescriptive character of evaluative discourse is derived from the writings of a number of British writers, in particular, R. M. Hare and P. H. Nowell-Smith. I have not, however, given detailed citations to their writings since my own discussion of this matter is carried on at an elementary level, and I would not want to charge either philosopher with responsibility for the views presented.

[2] Ludwig Wittgenstein, *Philosophical Investigations*, G. E. M. Anscombe (trans.), The Macmillan Company (New York, 1953), p. 20.

but nobody would suggest that it becomes a different tool as its use changes. We will avoid the dreary prospect of listing use after separate use of value judgments, if they, like hammers, have a basic character that accounts for the plurality of jobs they perform.

One particularly interesting place where value judgments find employment is in contexts of choice. In speaking of contexts of choice we need not restrict the discussion to cases where a person (or a group of persons) is facing an immediate decision concerning a line of action. The choice may have been made already, or may be expected to arise in the future. The choice can even be imaginary; we sometimes wonder how we should act in a situation hardly likely to arise: how should you act if you could become invisible at will? If you were God, what would you have people in Heaven do? But for the sake of simplicity, until further notice, I shall limit the discussion to contexts of real and immediate choice. It is in such contexts that we can study the prescriptive character of value judgments most easily.

Consider the following example as a case in point. You are out collecting tadpoles for a classroom display; you have a net full of them and you are picking out some and rejecting others. If the tadpoles are to be displayed before a large class of young children you will select large tadpoles and reject small tadpoles, and as soon as this criterion of choice has been established, a wide range of evaluative discourse becomes appropriate. Large tadpoles are called good; huge tadpoles are called excellent; small tadpoles are called bad; tiny tadpoles are called atrocious. In some other contexts the hierarchy could be reversed; if we wanted tadpoles that would show the entire process of development into a frog, the smaller a tadpole the better it would be.

Pointing out that evaluative discourse finds employment in contexts involving choice locates one arena of its activity, but does not tell us how it performs in this arena. This, then, is our next question: how do value judgments function in contexts involving choice; what role do they perform here? One way of approaching this question is to ask it in a slightly different fashion: what question (or questions) is answered by a value judgment in a context involving a choice? Or to give this a slight turn, if a value judgment is accepted, what questions no longer remain open?

We can begin by contrasting two kinds of questions; some are requests for directions, while others are requests for information.

The Prescriptive Force of Value Judgments

We request directions by means of a question such as: 'What am I to do?' or 'What is to be done?' If we are seeking information, we do so through some specification of the question, 'What is the case?' I shall say that expressions answering the first kind of question carry a *prescriptive force*, those which answer the second kind of question carry a *descriptive force*. *But these are not mutually exclusive categories*. If an expression carries one of these forces, it does not preclude the possibility that it carries the other force as well.

For the most part, sentences in the indicative mode carry a descriptive force. When I say 'Mikoyan is an Armenian' I am indicating that something is the case concerning Mikoyan, hence the sentence has a descriptive force. Virtually any sentence in the imperative carries a prescriptive force. The imperative 'Do such and such!' obviously answers the question 'What am I to do?'

I shall now put forth the modest claim that value judgments often, though not always, carry a prescriptive force. Since sentences in the imperative mode are the normal vehicle for prescriptive utterances, the same point can be made by saying that value judgments often function much like imperatives.[1] This is a convenient way of expressing the point provided that a number of misunderstandings are avoided. In the first place, I am not saying that value judgments *are* imperatives; they are, after all, indicatives. Nor am I saying that value judgments function exactly like imperatives; later we shall examine a number of important differences between imperatives and value judgments. Finally, imperatives should not be equated with commands, for a command is just one species of prescriptive discourse that can be expressed by a sentence in the imperative. A cookery book is composed mainly of imperatives, but usually contains no commands.

A number of writers have already substantiated the claim that value judgments have a prescriptive force,[2] and thus I shall merely illustrate this point rather than argue in detail on its behalf. Let us examine a context in which an imperative is used, and see how a value judgment can play a similar role in this

[1] Throughout, I have tried to use the term 'imperative' as the name for a kind of sentence (i.e. it is used as a grammatical category), while the term 'prescription' is a semantic category indicating a distinctive function. Thus 'prescription' stands in roughly the same relationship to 'imperative' as 'proposition' stands to 'declarative sentence'.

[2] Most notably, R. M. Hare.

context. The following conversation, though pedestrian, will serve our purposes:

A: Which pair of hiking boots shall I buy?

B: Buy the pair made in Austria![1]

B's reply gives a direct answer to A's request for directions, and hence, the imperative carries a prescriptive force. It would surely be odd for A to accept B's reply but still consider his question unanswered. Notice how paradoxical the following conversation appears:

A: Which pair of hiking boots shall I buy?

B: Buy the pair made in Austria!

A: All right, but still, which hiking boots shall I buy?

A's final remark is paradoxical because the words 'all right' signal that he has accepted B's directions while the remainder of the sentence suggests that he is still seeking directions.

The same paradoxical results arise if we substitute an appropriate value judgment for B's remark:

A: Which pair of hiking boots shall I buy?

B: The pair made in Austria are your best buy.

A: Granted, but still, which pair shall I buy?

Again, we would be at a loss to understand A's final remark. If he agrees that the boots made in Austria are *his* best buy, his question has been answered, and it makes no sense for him to ask it anew. Here we see a value judgment answering a request for directions, and thus, by our definition, it may be said to carry a prescriptive force. It is not yet clear *how* value judgments carry a prescriptive force, but none the less, it is worth noting that they sometimes do.

But value judgments need not carry the *strong* prescriptive force exhibited in the above example, i.e. they need not offer a *complete* answer to a question that is a request for directions. Notice that the following dialogue does make sense:

A: Which pair of hiking boots shall I buy?

B: Those made in Austria would be a good choice for you.

[1] I should really make an excuse for the trifling examples that I shall use. It would certainly be more exciting to examine the ethical ruminations of Antigone, but it would also lead to the endless repetition of the phrase 'setting aside the complicating factor . . .' Instead of levelling rich examples to the status of choosing between boots, I'll simply talk about choosing between boots to begin with.

A: Yes, but still, this Swiss pair looks awfully good; which pair shall I buy?

The conversation makes sense because B's reply leaves open the possibility that a better choice exists. If B had said that the Austrian boots were A's *best* choice, then A's final remark (even with the additional reference to the Swiss boots) would be hard to make out unless we take the word 'yes' as an expression of politeness and not an expression of assent. But even though B's reply does not give a *complete* answer to a question that is a request for directions, still it does offer a direct answer to such a question. To see this, notice that the following dialogue again has a peculiar ring:

A: Which pair of hiking boots shall I buy?
B: Those made in Austria would be a good choice for you.
A: Yes, of course, but now tell me something that is relevant to the question I just asked you.

These few examples illustrate that value judgments sometimes carry a prescriptive force by offering a direct answer to a request for directions. This does not show that these judgments always carry this force, and thus it would be presumptuous to take this single similarity between imperatives and evaluative statements as the basis for using the former as the model for analysing the latter. Furthermore, the idea of prescriptive force is far from clear. To bring this out, consider one further conversation:

A: Which pair of hiking boots shall I buy?
B: The ones made in Austria are the cheapest, soundest, and most comfortable.
A: Yes, of course, but now tell me something that is relevant to the question I just asked you.

Again A's final remark seems peculiar, for facts about cheapness, soundness, and comfort of the boots are precisely those facts that are relevant to the choice. None the less, A's remark is peculiar in a new way: it reveals a gross ignorance of the facts that are relevant to a choice, but it does not reveal gross ignorance concerning the status of a direct answer to a question.

In sum, I want to insist upon the difference between a statement that gives a direct answer to a request for directions and one that supplies information that is relevant for deciding what directions are reasonable. In the twilight zone between evaluative discourse and descriptive discourse this distinction is hard to maintain, and in § 11 of this chapter I shall try to make some sense out of these double-aspect terms. In any case, the distinction between giving a direct answer to a request for directions and giving relevant reasons that bear upon the giving of directions must be made good within the context of an otherwise satisfactory theory. For the moment it is only one piece of naïve data that could be interpreted in many ways.

3. TAKING STOCK

In the preceding chapter and in the opening sections of this chapter, I have come to accept three important theses concerning value judgments:

(1) Value judgments are assertions.
(2) Value judgments do not ascribe a material property to the thing evaluated.
(3) Value judgments often carry a prescriptive force, i.e. the force of an imperative.

Of these three theses, the second is the most suggestive, for if value judgments do not ascribe a material property to the thing evaluated, then perhaps they function to ascribe a warrant property, i.e. they assert something about a thing, but only indirectly, through making an assertion about the grounds on behalf of some further expression concerning that thing.

What sort of expression might a value judgment be about? The third thesis suggests an answer; since value judgments often carry a prescriptive force, value judgments could be assertions concerning the status of the grounds on behalf of a prescription. This suggestion ties all three theses together, for if value judgments are assertions concerning the status of available grounds on behalf of some prescription, then they are, after all, assertions, and thus the first thesis is accepted as well. I shall now present a warrant schema for value judgments, and following the pattern of Part One, start with a simple schema which will be progressively elaborated in order to account for some of the richness of evaluative discourse.

4. A WARRANT SCHEMA FOR VALUE JUDGMENTS

Let me begin with the example used in § 2, 'The hiking boots made in Austria are your best buy.' Under the warrant statement analysis, this remark concerns a certain line of action, the buying of a particular pair of hiking boots, by a particular person. I suggest the following as a warrant schema for this evaluative remark:

> There are adequate grounds on behalf of the prescription: Buy the Austrian hiking boots rather than any others.

I could make it explicitly clear that the prescription is directed to a particular person by rewriting it, '*You* buy the Austrian hiking boots rather than any other pair,' but presumably a person realizes it when a prescription is directed to him, and hence, it is cumbersome to point this out.

The very least we can expect from this pattern of analysis is that it squares with the facts used as the basis of its formulation, and the analysis I have presented has this much in its favour. The warrant statement is an assertion about a prescription, so it is an assertion. There would be nothing peculiar about calling a remark of this kind true or false, though it is not immediately clear what criteria would be used for deciding which to call it. The analysis also reflects the fact that value judgments, though assertions, do not give a direct description of the thing evaluated. The above analysis does not describe the hiking boots materially, it ascribes a warrant property by saying something about the grounds on behalf of a prescription concerning the hiking boots.

The most important fact is that this analysis carries the prescriptive force found in the value judgment operating in a context of choice. This can be best illustrated by returning to the logically peculiar conversation of § 2. We have seen that the following conversation makes little, if any, sense:

A: Which pair of hiking boots shall I buy?
B: The pair made in Austria is your best buy.
A: Granted, but still, which pair shall I buy?

If we substitute the appropriate analysis for B's remark, we get an equally senseless conversation:

A: Which pair of hiking boots shall I buy?
B: There are adequate grounds on behalf of the prescription: Buy the Austrian hiking boots rather than any other pair.
A: Granted, but still, which pair shall I buy?

This conversation is senseless because in accepting the claim that a prescription is adequately grounded, A accepts the prescription itself; and since the prescription gives a direct (and in this case, complete) answer to his question, it makes no sense for A to speak as if his question has gone unanswered. Thus the pattern of analysis squares with the three initial facts upon which it was based, and with this encouragement let us extend the pattern of analysis to include other evaluative terms, first of all, 'better' and 'good'.

Evaluative statements containing the term 'better' normally involve a comparison of two things.[1] This fact can be introduced into the pattern of analysis by adjusting the material component (i.e. the prescription) to make it clear that the range of choice is limited to just two things. Thus the evaluation 'A is better than B',[2] when used in a context of choice, may be interpreted as follows:

There are adequate grounds on behalf of the prescription: Choose A rather than B.

This is merely a special case of the pattern for 'A is the best ϕ' which can be represented as follows:

There are adequate grounds on behalf of the prescription: Choose A rather than any other ϕ.

Where only two things are involved, 'better' is equivalent to 'best'.

The prescriptive force of an evaluation employing the term 'better' varies with context. In contexts involving only two live options, such an evaluation has the same strong prescriptive

---

[1] I say normally, for 'better' is sometimes used to indicate 'superior to that available', for example, 'If you build a better mouse-trap, the world will beat a path to your door.'

[2] 'A is better than B' is an artificial locution for we almost always indicate in what way one thing is better than another. The use of expressions of this form, especially 'A is good' will give a stilted appearance to much of the discussion to follow, but it will cause, I believe, no systematic difficulties. I shall discuss the topic of kinds of value (or ways of being valuable) in §§ 10 and 11 of this chapter.

force as the claim that a thing is the best, while in contexts where more than two options are open, it carries less prescriptive force, for even if A is better than B, the decision to choose A may be overriden by the consideration that some further thing C is better yet. None the less, a claim that one thing is better than another carries some prescriptive force in a context of choice since it offers a direct, if not always complete, answer to a question that is a request for directions.

Evaluations involving the terms 'better' and 'best' introduce a specific ordering relationship with respect to things evaluated. This isn't normally so for evaluations that employ the term 'good', unless it is qualified by some such adjective as 'greatest' or 'highest'. Subject to certain qualifications, let me suggest the following warrant schema for evaluations involving the term 'good':

There are adequate grounds in behalf of the prescription: Choose A.

Here it should be understood that the grounds do not include comparative matters; there are adequate grounds for choosing A *as such*, but perhaps *not* adequate grounds for choosing A rather than some other thing B. This leaves open the possibility that A is not the best thing in the context of choice, and even that there are many things that are better; but these are just the possibilities that we wish to leave open when we call something good.

The prescriptive force of value judgments involving the term 'good' will vary greatly in strength. In a context in which the options are merely between choosing A rather than rejecting A, then the claim that A is good will have the highest prescriptive force. In a context where A is simply one choice among many others, calling it good can have the effect (and intended effect) of damning with faint praise. As always, it is only in a concrete context that the prescriptive force will be determined, and even in a concrete context the term 'good' may offer only a general and indefinite commendation.

The three positive evaluative terms I have discussed are paired off with negative evaluative terms in the following fashion:

good	bad
better	worse
best	worst

These negative evaluative terms can be brought under the pattern of analysis through the simple device of employing a negative prescription in the material component:

A is bad = There are adequate grounds on behalf of the prescription: Do not choose A.[1]

A is worse than B = There are adequate grounds on behalf of the prescription: Choose B rather than A.

A is the worst ϕ = There are adequate grounds on behalf of the prescription: Choose any ϕ rather than A.

A detailed examination of the logical relationships between this entire family of evaluative terms will be the subject of § 6.

5. SOME POINTS OF CLARIFICATION

The analysis has been extended to include the terms 'good', 'better', 'best', and their opposites, 'bad', 'worse', and 'worst'. These analyses are here collected for the convenience of future reference.

A is good = There are adequate grounds on behalf of the prescription: Choose A.

A is bad = There are adequate grounds on behalf of the prescription: Do not choose A.

A is better than B = There are adequate grounds on behalf of the prescription: Choose A rather than B.

A is worse than B = There are adequate grounds on behalf of the prescription: Choose B rather than A.

A is the best ϕ = There are adequate grounds on behalf of the prescription: Choose A rather than any other ϕ.

A is the worst ϕ = There are adequate grounds on behalf of the prescription: Choose any ϕ rather than A.

[1] Again, as in the case of evaluations involving the term 'good', these grounds will not include reference to comparison with other objects. 'Bad' is a general and indefinite term of condemnation.

Some Points of Clarification

Each of these analyses involves a warrant component ranging over a prescription, and the specific differences are explained by the nature of the prescription contained in each.

There are three features of this pattern of analysis which need explanation: (1) the character of the warrant component must be clarified; (2) the meaning of the term 'choose' in the material component needs explication; and (3) the relationship between the warrant component and the material component must be delineated.

(1) In Part One the warrant component was formulated in the phrase 'there are adequate grounds available on behalf of the *assertion*', and, of course, this wording is no longer suitable now that prescriptions are admitted as the material component of a warrant statement. We could correct this by replacing the word 'assertion' by the word 'expression'—using this latter word to cover both assertions and prescriptions—but instead of taking this course, I shall continue to employ the word 'prescription' in order to underscore the prescriptive character of evaluative discourse.

An examination of the warrant component will also give rise to a more important consideration. When presented with a proposed analysis of value judgments the critic will immediately ask if the analysis itself employs any evaluative terms, and if it does, he will then ask for the analysis of all the evaluative terms within the analysis. The embarrassing result of trying to meet this demand would be an infinite regress of analyses within analyses. The suspicious word—and it seems to me the only suspicious word—in this pattern of analysis is 'adequate', and in point of fact, I am willing to admit that this word can be given an evaluative interpretation.

To see our way out of this difficulty we must reflect upon the role played by the term 'adequate' in the warrant component. This term provides one filling for the variable 'ϕ' in the schema of the warrant component:

There are ϕ grounds of a θ kind in behalf of . . .

This variable is intended to provide a way of indicating the *degree* of evidential support that the grounds in question lend to the material component. The notion of adequacy was specifically introduced as a way of indicating that from the given grounds the material component is established. It is only natural that we sometimes use evaluative terms that assess these grounds in virtue of their capacity to lend evidential support to the material component instead of stating explicitly just what the degree of evidential support in fact is. Thus, instead of saying that the material reasons lend a high degree of probability to some conclusion, we might say that we have quite good reasons in behalf of this conclusion. In sum, reasons themselves can become subject to evaluation in virtue of their capacity to lend support to some conclusion, but we are under no compulsion to use evaluative terms in the warrant schemata for evaluative statements.

My suggestion, then, is this: warrant claims indicate various degrees of support that a set of grounds can give to some further expression, be it an assertion or prescription. Warrant claims have a more fundamental status than evaluations, for evaluation emerges when warranting claims are applied to prescriptions. This point is not overturned by the fact that grounds themselves can become subject to evaluation in virtue of their capacity to lend evidential support, for this merely shows that a warrant claim can itself become the subject of a warrant claim. Thus one form of the infinite regress problem remains. We may be called upon endlessly to give reasons in behalf of our reasons, and we may also be called upon to make good our claim that the reasons we have in mind lend that degree of support that we assign to them. These, however, are not problems generated by the warrant statement approach; they are facts of life that the approach should reflect.

(2) The use of the term 'choose' in the prescriptions is unfortunate, for it might suggest that all evaluations are concerned with taking physical possession of an object. I do not wish to use the concept in this narrow sense: under choosing I shall include all those modes of action that are *for* a thing and under the heading of not choosing (or rejecting) I shall include all those modes of action that are *against* a thing. This corresponds roughly to the distinction Hobbes draws between *towards* and *fromwards* motions, though the spatial character (and dubious psychology) of his concepts is avoided. Thus under the heading of choosing I shall include such diverse activities as buying, tasting, seizing, joining, etc. A similar disparate list can be drawn up for not choosing (or rejecting).[1]

---

[1] I am using the term 'choose' in the same wide sense that Ralph Barton Perry uses the term 'interest' in his *General Theory of Value*.

(3) The relationship between the warrant component and the prescription in the material component can cause a further difficulty. Someone might argue that it makes no sense to say that a sound argument can be offered on behalf of a prescription, for only assertions can serve as the proper conclusion to an argument. I fail to see the force of this criticism. It would, of course, be nonsense to say that a prescription, when it takes the form of an imperative, can be verified, i.e. shown to be true, but I am not suggesting that imperatives can be verified, only that they can be justified, and since the process of justifying an imperative is entirely familiar, I cannot see why it should be considered suspect.

The above answer is a bit glib, but I hardly know what else to say. Perhaps the reason the notion of justifying a prescription sounds odd is related to the fact that people engaged in theoretical enterprises (such as philosophy) spend much time defending assertions, and relatively less time defending imperatives. Because of this, it becomes natural to assume that the function of all argument is to establish *truth*. If, however, the reader reflects upon such activities as offering advice, or giving directions, I think he will see it is also possible to present arguments on behalf of imperatives. If an appeal to an august authority will help: Immanuel Kant had no qualms about offering arguments on behalf of his Categorical Imperative, which, after all, was an imperative.

Finally, it is entirely arbitrary to insist that whenever we seem to be defending an imperative, we are in fact defending an assertion, insisting, for example, that a defence of the imperative 'Do such and such' is really a defence of the assertion 'You ought to do such and such'. This is just as arbitrary as insisting that whenever we attempt to defend an assertion we are really defending an imperative of the form 'Believe such and such!'

6. SOME IMPORTANT LOGICAL ISOMORPHISMS

The following three pairs of squares of opposition exhibit an exact logical isomorphism. In each case, the top square consists of a family of evaluative terms in the natural language, while the bottom square presents the respective warrant schemata:[1]

(1) Good and Bad (where the decision concerns choosing or rejecting A):

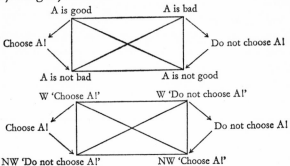

(2) Better and Worse (where a choice is being made between A and B):

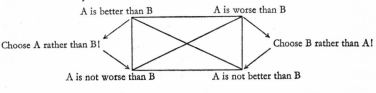

(3) Best and Worst (where a choice is being made between various ϕ):

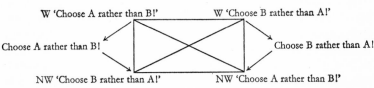

[1] The stipulation is still in force that we are restricting our attention to contexts involving a real and immediate choice. Furthermore, for each pair of squares of opposition a further stipulation has been introduced that limits the range of choices to give the contraries a strong prescriptive force. These limitations are needed to guarantee the status of the imperatives that play the role of intermediate expressions. These intermediate expressions will be discussed in detail in the next chapter.

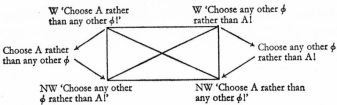

W 'Choose A rather than any other φ!' W 'Choose any other φ rather than A!'

Choose A rather than any other φ

Choose any other φ rather than A!

NW 'Choose any other φ rather than A!' NW 'Choose A rather than any other φ!'

Thus, there is a perfect logical isomorphism between the squares of opposition for these evaluative statements and the squares of opposition for their corresponding warrant schemata. And these isomorphisms go beyond the relationships found on the squares of opposition. Let me present a few examples. If A is better than B, then it does not follow that A is good, and similarly, the claim that there are adequate grounds for choosing A rather than B does not entail that there are adequate grounds for choosing A. A slightly more complicated example runs as follows: If A is the best φ, and B is a φ distinct from A, then we can infer that A is better than B. Similarly, if there are adequate grounds for choosing A rather than any other φ, and B is a φ distinct from A, then we can infer that there are adequate grounds for choosing A rather than B. As far as I know, there are no counter-examples to this logical isomorphism between these evaluative statements and their appropriate warrant schemata.

But even if this logical isomorphism does exist, this will not show that the suggested pattern of analysis is correct; syntactical isomorphism is a necessary, but not a sufficient, condition for the soundness of a given pattern of analysis. In point of fact, this is a very weak criterion of adequacy that can be met by systems of statements that have little or nothing else in common with evaluative statements.[1] Yet even if this is a weak criterion of adequacy, it provides us with a test that a proposed pattern of analysis can fail; and I will here state dogmatically that this criterion has not been met by any pattern of analysis hitherto suggested,[2] and it is for this reason that I have gone through

[1] Other warrant statements show a striking similarity to value judgments, but for that matter, so do quantified statements and many statements involving relations. Any asymmetrical relationship (such as taller than) will generate a square of opposition, though not always with intermediate propositions.

[2] In many cases, a proposed pattern of analysis can be rejected out of hand simply because it cannot exhibit good and bad as *logical* contraries. If, for example, goodness is identified with the sensation of pleasure, and badness is identified with a distinct sensation of pain, then good and bad will not be logical contraries; at best, they will be empirically exclusive properties.

the tedious business of showing that the warrant statement analysis of value judgments at least seems to meet this criterion.

7. THE INTERMEDIATE IMPERATIVES FOR EVALUATIVE STATEMENTS

In the preceding section I glossed over a point that may have caused the reader some uneasiness; it may not seem entirely obvious that the imperatives that play the role of intermediate expressions[1] stand in the designated entailment relationships between the strong and weak propositions. Consider the following entailment statement as a case in point:

'A is better than B' entails 'Choose A rather than B'.

I can think of two possible objections to this statement: (1) it makes no sense at all to say that an assertion entails an imperative; and (2) such an entailment statement makes sense, but this one (and the others cited in the previous section) does not happen to be correct.

(1) As a point of grammar, the first objection is sound enough. We normally speak about something entailing (or implying) that . . ., where the word 'that' introduces some propositional matter. Thus to allow an imperative to be entailed by anything, even another imperative, involves an extension of ordinary language. But if we return to the traditional notion that when one thing entails another, the second thing must be contained in the first, this extension will not seem unreasonable. Admittedly, the notion of containment is both metaphorical and vague, but still, we have seen that a value judgment often carries the prescriptive force of an imperative, i.e. gives a direct answer to a question that an imperative answers directly. It is in this sense that a value judgment contains an imperative, and it is in this sense that I shall say a value judgment entails an imperative. I can put matters in the following way: in a context involving a choice between A and B, if we can legitimately assert that A is better than B, then we can (under certain conditions) also legitimately prescribe choosing A rather than B.

(2) The second objection, that these entailments make sense, but just do not happen to hold, can arise for two possible reasons:

---

[1] We must now use the more general name 'intermediate expression' rather than 'intermediate proposition' since imperatives are now playing this role.

(i) forgetting the stipulation that the discussion is limited to contexts involving a genuine choice; or (ii) using different grounds in assessing the evaluation and the imperative.

(i) There are, of course, any number of contexts in which value judgments do not carry a prescriptive force since no choice is being made between possible lines of conduct. Past tense value judgments,[1] for example, carry only indirect (and sometimes no) prescriptive force. Notice, however, that for each pair of squares of opposition a specific stipulation has been made indicating a determinate context of choice, and it is only counter-examples drawn from the designated contexts that can count against these squares of opposition.

(ii) But, someone might argue, even in a context of choice, it sometimes makes sense to tell a person not to choose the better of two things. The Cadillac, everyone would admit, is a better car than the Ford, yet acknowledging this, we still might tell a person to choose a Ford rather than a Cadillac. This, of course, is well taken, but notice that the reasons (the material reasons) that we would offer in defence of the evaluation, 'The Cadillac is a better car than the Ford,' would be quite different from the reasons we would offer in support of the prescription, 'Choose a Ford rather than a Cadillac.' We might say that a Cadillac is a better car, yet the Ford is a better *buy* (if buying is the kind of choice at issue). In common parlance, we can avoid confusions concerning the kind of material reasons at issue by using such phrasing as: 'The Ford is a better car *for you* than the Cadillac,' and here the phrase 'for you' indicates that the assessment takes into account the particular circumstances of a given person. I suggest that no counter-examples will be found to the entailment relationships between evaluations and imperatives if the stipulation concerning the context of choice is kept in mind, and if the character of the material grounds is held constant. In point of fact, however, value judgments find employment in contexts where neither of these restrictions is in force. Their character under such circumstances is the subject of the next section.

8. THE VARIABILITY OF PRESCRIPTIVE FORCE

In § 2 of this chapter, I laid down the stipulation that the discussion be limited to contexts involving an immediate and

---

[1] Past tense value judgments will be discussed in more detail in the next section.

genuine choice concerning the thing evaluated, and in the preceding section I laid down the additional restriction that the grounds for the value judgment must be the same as those for the prescription. With these restrictions in force it was possible to produce a simple account of the prescriptive character of evaluative discourse. I shall now remove both of these restrictions and try to show that the warrant schemata will fail to carry prescriptive force in just those contexts in which evaluations fail to carry prescriptive force.

To begin with, the discussion of the evaluation of things (as opposed to the evaluation of the *choice* of things) has been plainly artificial. Usually, when I say that x is the best ϕ I am indicating that there are grounds of a *standard sort* available for choosing x rather than any other ϕ. In saying that the grounds are *standard*, I mean, of course, that they concern those factors that are relevant to just about anyone making a choice between ϕs. Thus I may agree that x is the best ϕ, yet be unwilling to agree that x is *my best* choice. I may reject this claim on the trivial grounds that I am not interested in choosing between various ϕs, but more significantly, I may reject it because certain special considerations override the standard considerations invoked in the value judgment 'x is the best ϕ'. I may agree, for example, that the Volkswagen is a splendid car, but refuse to buy one simply because of a lingering resentment towards the Germans.

Value judgments of this sort (i.e. value judgments that indicate the status of standard backing for some prescription) perform a useful service in the language. If we command a stock of such judgments, we can approach a situation of choice with at least part of the assessment in hand and thus be relieved of the task of going back to material reasons at every point in the assessment. Since there can be a difference between standard grounds and the specific grounds of a given context, there is no simple way of characterizing the prescriptive force of this kind of value judgment.[1] Roughly speaking, the prescriptive force of these evaluations depends upon the relevance of standard considerations to a given context.

Tenses introduce further complications concerning prescriptive force. Consider the following remark as a case in point.

[1] Simplicity is lost because we here allow a disparity between the grounds for the value judgment and the grounds for the prescription.

> It was better for Caesar to cross the Rubicon quickly rather than to wait and allow his enemies to consolidate their position.

This remark is about a choice, a choice that confronted Caesar, but in this context the evaluation carries no direct prescriptive force; it gives directions to no one. It surely gives no directions to Caesar, for it would be idle, if not senseless, to direct instructions into the past. We shall see that past tense evaluations can have indirect prescriptive force, but on the very face of it, past tense evaluations are about the past, and do not offer prescriptions for present activity.

If we substitute the appropriate warrant schema for this remark, again the prescriptive force is lacking:

> There were, at the time, adequate grounds in behalf of the prescription: Caesar, cross the Rubicon quickly, etc.!

This rendition of the original is surely stilted, and it will sound all the more stilted if we read the prescription as a command and then wonder who it is that is addressing a command to Caesar. But the material component does not formulate a piece of dialogue, and therefore it is out of place even to ask who it is that is issuing this prescription. In this respect, prescriptions must be accorded the same privileges that have traditionally been accorded to propositions.

Furthermore, we sometimes employ value judgments in hypothetical or imaginary matters of choice, and once more such evaluations lack a direct prescriptive force:

> If Russia were invaded by men from Mars, it would be better for the United States to join forces with Russia than to let her fight alone.

The corresponding and again stilted warrant statement analysis of this remark takes the following form:

> If Russia were invaded by men from Mars, there would then be adequate grounds in behalf of the prescription: United States, join forces with Russia, etc.

Evaluations admit of a past tense, and for that matter, admit of all tenses and moods, and this creates difficulties for a theory that identifies value judgments with some kind of imperative. Indeed, I think these difficulties are insuperable; by using the imperative as the model for evaluative discourse an account can be given of the contexts in which value judgment *do* carry a prescriptive force, but it seems impossible to make sense out of those contexts in which value judgments *do not* carry a prescriptive force. No such difficulties are encountered on the warrant statement approach to evaluations. Tenses and moods are provided for by incorporating the following such phrases in the warrant component:

> There *are* grounds.
> There *were* grounds.
> There *will* be grounds.
> There *may be* grounds.
> There *could be* grounds.
> There *would have been* grounds.
> There *might have been* grounds.
> etc.

This provision for tenses and moods helps to account for the variability in prescriptive force of evaluative statements.

Though past tense and contrary-to-fact evaluations do not carry a direct prescriptive force, they sometimes do so indirectly; if the thing evaluated in the past or imagined case is significantly similar to a present option, then the evaluation will have an indirect prescriptive force for the present case. The reasoning runs as follows: ϕ was (or would be) good; θ is just like ϕ; therefore θ is good. Since the evaluation 'θ is good' can have a direct prescriptive force, 'θ was good' can have this prescriptive force indirectly.[1] This reasoning involves a principle that is sometimes expressed by saying that value is a *consequential* or *resultant* property. By this it is meant that the value of a thing is always determined by its other non-value properties, and thus, value cannot vary independently of them. From this it follows that things that are the same with respect to certain properties will have the same value with respect to these properties. It is through this doctrine that a value judgment about a past or imagined case can bear upon a present decision and thus have an indirect prescriptive force.

The consequential character of value is accounted for by the

---

[1] I insist that this prescriptive force is indirect because the value judgment is, after all, about the past.

pattern of analysis here presented. If in a given context the facts warrant a particular prescription, then the same prescription is again warranted in a new context where the facts are in no way significantly different. It makes no sense to say that A and B are exactly alike in every respect, including contextual relationships, but A is good and B is not. It makes just as little sense to say that A and B are alike in every respect, including contextual relationships, but a particular prescription involving A is warranted and that the same prescription involving B is not.

The ability of the proposed pattern of analysis to make sense out of the consequential character of value is a strong point in its favour, for as an ontological category the notion of a consequential property leads to mystery; how, we are led to wonder, can a set of factual properties cause this very different kind of property to come into existence? But no mystery is involved in saying that a set of properties can warrant a prescription concerning a thing. To say that a bicycle's broken sprocket warrants our not buying it is thoroughly intelligible, but saying that this fact causes the bicycle to have the consequential property of instrumental disvalue turns a simple fact into a philosophical puzzle.

9. A RECAPITULATION

Since this chapter has been long, arid, and technical, let me summarize the results obtained thus far. I have presented three lines of argument in order to create a strong presumption in favour of a warrant statement analysis of value judgments involving the terms:

good	bad
better	worse
best	worst

(1) The pattern of analysis squares with the three theses presented earlier in the chapter:

(i) Value judgments are assertions.

(ii) Value judgments do not ascribe a material property to the thing evaluated.

(iii) Value judgments sometimes carry a prescriptive force, i.e. the force of an imperative.

As far as I know, this is the only pattern of analysis that conforms to all three of these theses at once.

(2) I have tried to show that a logical isomorphism exists between evaluative statements and their corresponding warrant schemata. Furthermore, I suggest that the warrant statement approach helps us to better understand the logical relationships between evaluative statements.

(3) Finally, these four striking parallels exist between evaluations and the pattern of analysis with respect to prescriptive force:

(i) Both evaluations and their appropriate analyses can carry a prescriptive force in a context of choice.

(ii) The strength of the prescriptive force of evaluations varies with the character of the evaluation and the nature of the context, and this variation is reflected in the appropriate analyses.

(iii) In some contexts, evaluations carry no prescriptive force, and here the appropriate analyses lack this force as well.

(iv) In some contexts, evaluations carry a prescriptive force only indirectly, and here again the pattern of analysis maintains a parallel.

Now, following the pattern first used for alethic modalities in Chapter II, I shall extend this pattern of analysis to cover first, *kinds* of goodness (or value), and then, *degrees* of goodness (or value). This will lay the foundation for the closing chapter where I shall discuss the bearing of warrant statement analysis upon a number of philosophical problems concerning value.

10. KINDS OF VALUE

The six evaluative terms that I have thus far discussed have this in common: there seem to be no limitations upon their range of application. They not only can be applied to every sort of object, they can also be applied to every sort of category; we speak of a good deed, a good person, a good character, a good location, a good posture, etc. Furthermore, these terms can be applied to the same thing in a number of different ways: we can adjudge Socrates a good philosopher but a bad provider. I shall mark the promiscuous character of these six evaluative terms by saying that they are *topic neutral*.

Kinds of Value

It is precisely because of this topic neutrality that these six evaluative terms are called upon so often, but at first glance this would seem to lead to hopeless confusion, for if these terms can be applied on any sort of grounds, what determinate information can they give? As a matter of fact, the topic neutrality of these six terms does sometimes cause confusion, but in a large measure, confusion is avoided by a simple grammatical device: though these terms function adjectively, they almost never directly modify the thing evaluated, and the thing they do modify indicates what kinds of grounds are at issue. Thus we would hardly say that Woodrow Wilson was good,[1] instead, we would say that he was a good college president, a good husband, a good leader of his party, a good Christian, and so on; and in each case the noun modified by the word 'good' indicates the kind of evaluation being made. When there is no suitable class term available for specifying the kind of grounds at issue, other more complex locutions can perform the same task; for example, 'Woodrow Wilson was not *good at* getting his measures through a hostile Senate.' Such locutions as 'good at', 'good for', and 'good as' allow us to specify the character of the grounds of an evaluation in whatever detail that is necessary. And, of course, a more direct procedure for indicating the kind of value in question is to modify the evaluative adjective directly with an adverb. Thus we speak of things being aesthetically good, politically good, economically good, etc.[2]

In order to provide for these different kinds of value—for these different ways of being good—we can employ the same type of warrant component that was used for kinds of necessity:

> There are adequate grounds *of a kind* θ available for the prescription: . . .

Thus to say that Woodrow Wilson was a good president indicates that he adequately meets the standards used in judging presidents. Since the overwhelming majority of evaluative statements will contain a grammatical device for specifying the kinds of grounds

[1] We would only say this if it were completely clear what kind of grounds are at issue. In response to the explicit question 'How was Wilson at presiding over cabinet meetings?' 'He was good' could be appropriate.

[2] A recent innovation is the indiscriminate use of the suffix '-wise', for example, 'The President's health has improved, heart condition-wise.'

163

at issue, their warrant statement analyses will have to include this reference to the kind of grounds in the warrant component.

I might here repeat that much of the previous discussion in this chapter has had a curiously artificial ring simply because the examples employed value judgments that left the character of the evaluation unspecified. The claim that a Ford is better than a Cadillac sounds incomplete, for we want to ask 'Better in what respect?' and until this question is answered we hardly know what to think about the assertion. I can only plead an inability to discuss everything at once as the reason for using these stilted examples.

11. TOPIC BOUND EVALUATIVE TERMS

There are any number of grammatical devices that allow us to restrict topic neutral evaluative terms to a particular mode of evaluation, and I shall make no attempt to catalogue them; instead, I shall discuss another class of evaluative terms that performs a double function of evaluating and indicating the kind of grounds employed in the evaluation. These are the evaluative terms that find employment only in special regions, and hence I have called them *topic bound evaluative terms*.

As an example, consider the word 'delicious'. Saying that something is delicious is to make a remark concerning its taste, but the term 'delicious' is not the name of any particular taste. Here we have the basis for a dialectical development. On G. E. Moore's approach, deliciousness would surely emerge as a non-natural property and we would be faced with any number of insuperable difficulties. Deliciousness is certainly related to the empirical taste of a thing, but it would seem impossible to make sense out of the nature of the relationship. Furthermore, how is deliciousness related to the other non-natural properties of goodness? There must be some close relationship, for saying that something *tastes good* comes to much the same thing as saying that it is delicious. Is there just one property of goodness that we call by the name delicious when it happens to get associated with a taste and by some other name when associated with other things —something like one God called by different names in different lands? Or are we to give some other account of the relationships between various species of value?

On the emotivist approach we would have to say that 'delicious' is simply the conventional word for expressing a favourable attitude towards the taste of a food. As such the claim that a piece of pie is delicious gives us no verifiable information about the pie—a curious doctrine, for if we know that the apples have turned rotten, this *fact* will constitute obvious counter-evidence to the claim that the pie is delicious. We can, I think, reconstruct the entire controversy about the meaning of the term 'good', using the term 'delicious' in its place. Such a reconstruction would represent a powerful *reductio ad absurdum* of this debate.

The word 'delicious' presents no special problems for the warrant statement approach; in fact, the warrant component making reference to the *kinds* of grounds introduced in the preceding section will do half the job; giving a clearer specification of the prescriptive component should complete it. The following is a rough, perhaps a very rough, translation of the sentence, 'X is delicious.'

> There are adequate grounds, of a kind respecting flavour, available on behalf of the prescription: Taste X.

In a context in which the tasting or not tasting of X are the only options, and flavour is the only basis for a decision, this remark (and corresponding analysis of it) carries the strong prescriptive force of the imperative 'Taste X!'; in a context where there are other options (perhaps things that are even more delicious) or additional criteria for evaluation (perhaps caloric considerations), then the remark and its corresponding analysis carry a weaker prescriptive force.

I have used the term 'delicious' as an initial example of a topic bound evaluative word because it is possible to give a fairly plausible warrant statement interpretation of assertions that employ it, and it is not a term that has been the centre of philosophical controversy. A more interesting example would be the term 'beautiful', for I think that evaluations that involve this term also conform to the pattern:

> There are adequate grounds, of a kind θ, available on behalf of the prescription: Choose X.

I do not want, however, to give the impression that the variables in this pattern can be replaced in a routine fashion. Quite the contrary. Filling in the θ and the character of the choosing would demand the construction of an entire aesthetic theory.

I have no desire to go on listing terms that perform this double function of evaluating and indicating what kind of evaluation is being made, nor do I propose to offer detailed warrant schemata for statements involving such terms,[1] but I shall give some idea of the diversity of such terms in the English language. The whole range of terms with the suffix '-worthy' function in this way. If I say that a ship is seaworthy, the suffix indicates an evaluation, the stem marks off the kind of evaluation. Many terms with the suffix '-able' function in the same way. And not all evaluative terms are adjectives; if I call someone a bridge *expert*, the term introduces the evaluation, while the term 'bridge' indicates the nature of the evaluation. The English language—and I imagine every other language—provides unending ways of ascribing warrant properties that bear upon various lines of conduct, i.e. unending ways of evaluating things.

12. DEONTIC MODALITIES

I propose to treat the terms that are associated with 'right'—the so-called deontic modalities—as a special kind of region-bound evaluative terms. The distinctive mark of these terms is that they are normally restricted in their use to the evaluation of acts or act-types. This is reflected in their grammar, for we often use such phrasing as: 'it is wrong to . . .', 'you are obliged to . . .', 'it is your duty to . . .', 'it was right to . . .', etc., where the blank is filled in with an expression indicating an act or an act-type. Deontic modal terms are not always followed by verbs in the infinitive; participial constructions are also common (e.g. 'Stealing is wrong'), but here again it is a kind of act or act-type that is evaluated. These terms are region bound then because they are normally limited in their application to a given category: acts or act-types.

Notice that deontic modal terms are region bound in a different sense from, for example, the term 'delicious'. The term 'delicious', except when used metaphorically, indicates that an evaluation is

---

[1] This is a subtle enterprise, and it is very easy to make errors concerning the most obvious evaluative terms. Furthermore, let me repeat that I am not particularly interested in drawing distinctions between closely related kinds of warrant statements, and I would only clutter up the text with errors of detail if I were to try. I might remark, however, that much of Nowell-Smith's discussion (in his *Ethics*) of A-words and G-words can be taken over for filling out warrant schemata.

made with respect to flavour. From this it follows that it can be applied to only those things that have a flavour—there are no delicious theorems in geometry, and no delicious states of character. In contrast, a term such as 'right' gives no indication of the *kind* of grounds that are at issue. This is worth noting, for there is a temptation to think that words such as 'right' and 'ought' have a distinctive moral quality, which, as a matter of fact, they do not possess. Deontic terms are limited in their application to acts or act-types, but as far as specifying the nature of the grounds available on behalf of a prescription, they are every bit as topic neutral as the terms 'good' and 'bad'.

There are no difficulties in applying the warrant statement analysis to deontic statements, and, if anything, it seems more immediately plausible in this domain than for evaluations of the kind discussed earlier. Deontic statements, especially those employing the term 'ought', often have the ring of an imperative. If I say, 'Charles, you ought to visit your grandmother', I am plainly telling him to visit his grandmother. Furthermore, the warrant statement approach gives some account of the authoritative quality of ought-statements. If I use the naked imperative, 'Charles, visit your grandmother!', this may be taken as a command, and perhaps I have no right to direct commands to Charles. If, on the other hand, I use the more polite imperative, 'Charles, please visit your grandmother!', it sounds as if I am asking a favour. But if I inform him that there are adequate grounds, perhaps adequate moral grounds, available for the prescription, 'Charles, visit your grandmother!', then it is plain that I am not asking a favour nor am I uttering a command; I am making, I suggest, just the authoritative remark that is expressed by an ought-statement.

The only technical difficulty is finding some way of constructing a warrant schema that reflects the fact that it is an act-type or act that is evaluated. We could use the cumbersome phrase 'Choose doing so and so!' and thereby indicate that is it a kind of *doing* that is being evaluated. But instead of saying 'Choose doing', we would more naturally say 'Do', and using this phraseology we can employ the following warrant schema for deontic statements:

There are adequate grounds available of a kind θ for the prescription: *Do* such and such!

With this warrant schema we can give an account of the following square of opposition:

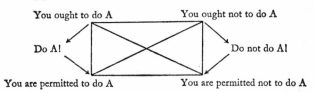

You ought to do A   You ought not to do A

Do A!   Do not do A!

You are permitted to do A   You are permitted not to do A

Again the inferences hold only if the grounds are held constant throughout.[1] The contraries 'right–wrong' and 'obliged–forbidden' yield two further squares of opposition where again all standard relationships hold on the proviso that the grounds of assessment are held constant.

I shall not here attempt to characterize the *differences* between various deontic terms; once more I shall avoid the pitfalls involved in sorting out closely related warrant statements. Important work has been done in this area by E. J. Lemmon, and I think that many of his results can be taken over for the construcion of specific warrant schemata for deontic statements.[2] I am not, however, entirely sure how this would work out in detail.

13. THE RIGHT AND THE GOOD

There is a tradition of dividing evaluative terms into two broad categories; the first includes the term 'good' and its kin (terms that supposedly evaluate the ends or objects of action), the second includes those terms that cluster about the word 'right' (terms that supposedly evaluate actions themselves). This distinction forms the basis of the dispute between the deontologists and teleologists who divide over which category is to be considered fundamental.

I shall not argue, as the reader might expect, that this dispute is merely a linguistic muddle masquerading as a substantive issue. I do think that the general confusion concerning the character of evaluative discourse has made it virtually impossible to deal

---

[1] In live contexts the inference from an A ought-statement to the imperative is often blocked precisely because there are grounds independent of those invoked by the ought-statement that bear upon the proposed line of conduct. Thus, for example, I can accept a *prudential* ought yet reject the prescription it contains because I find the prescription *morally* unwarranted.

[2] 'Moral Dilemmas', *The Philosophical Review*, vol. LXXI, No. 2 (April 1962).

with this dispute in an intelligible fashion, but even after the linguistic confusion has been cleared away, there remains a problem that is both difficult and important. At rock bottom, the dispute comes to this: what kind of *material reasons* are fundamental in moral assessment, those that concern the relationship of an act to a system of laws, rules, or principles; or those that concern the value of the effects that the act will have upon the world?[1] The deontologist gives priority to deontic statements because we typically use such statements for the assessment of acts with respect to rules, laws, or principles; the teleologist, in turn, gives first place to those locutions that are used in evaluating the effects of action.

It should be clear that (and why) warrant statement analysis cannot offer a solution to this dispute. The claim that evaluative statements tell us about the status of the material reasons available for some prescription, leaves entirely open all questions concerning the content of these material reasons. Here there is an exact parallel with probability statements. No analysis of the statement 'It is highly probable that there is life on Mars' will reveal what it is that *makes* life on Mars highly probable. Similarly, no analysis of 'Stealing is wrong' will show us what *makes* stealing wrong. To use an older terminology, no examination of the meaning of the term 'right' will show us what properties are right-making.

If the reader finds the above results disappointing—or if he takes them to show the paucity of the method here employed, I can only say that they are precisely the results that one would expect. Just as the astronomer cannot settle empirical questions through reflecting upon the meaning of such terms as 'nebula' or 'super nova', the philosopher cannot settle substantive issues in ethics through merely reflecting upon the meaning of the terms that are used in formulating these issues. All such attempts have been dialectical in Kant's pejorative sense of that word.

14. DEGREES OF VALUE

The most direct way of dealing with degrees of value—with things that are very good, fairly good, hardly any good at all, etc.—is to view them as implicit comparisons and then treat them

---

[1] There is no reason to suppose that these are the only considerations that are relevant to moral appraisal; it's simply a fact that philosophers have made the greatest fuss over these two.

along lines introduced in § 4 of this chapter. For example, the claim that something is a very good ϕ could be taken as roughly equivalent to the assertion that it is a better ϕ than most, and then the warrant schema for evaluations involving 'better than' would become appropriate. There would certainly be problems of detail in translating statements concerning degrees of value into statements about comparative value, but none of these problems would seem to raise systematic difficulties for the warrant statement approach.

15. THE INTERCHANGE OF EVALUATIVE TERMS WITH OTHER WARRANT TERMS

I have already remarked upon our tendency to transfer warrant terms from one area to another; for example, we sometimes use the verb 'to see' as an epistemic term. Here, the most interesting interchange is between alethic modalities and deontic modalities, an interchange that goes in both directions. Thus the remark:

It is necessary to operate immediately.

is a deontic statement; it indicates that a certain line of action ought to be pursued. On the other hand, the following ought-statement functions as an alethic modal statement:

That ought to fix it.

Here we would hardly be ascribing some obligation to the referent of 'that' (which is probably something like tightening a screw); instead, we are indicating that the prediction 'It is fixed' is well grounded. It would be possible to give any number of examples of this interchange between strong alethic modal terms and strong deontic terms, but I shall stop by simply mentioning that the verbs 'must' and 'have to' perform both functions. The term 'may' is a weak warrant word that functions both to indicate possibility and permission.

We may also notice an important *difference* between alethic modalities and deontic modalities. If we use the somewhat artificial phrasing 'It ought to be the case that p' and 'It is necessarily the case that p', symbolizing them respectively as 'Op' and '$\Box p$', we find that $\Box p$ entails p, but that Op does not entail p. This difference is just what we should expect, for under analysis

'□p' contains the assertion 'p' as its material component while 'Op' does not. We can then look to the shared warrant component for an explanation of the similarities between alethic logic and deontic logic and to the differing material components for an explanation of dissimilarities.

If we turn now to the epistemic and perceptual modalities, we find that they occur in such expressions as 'seeing how' and 'knowing how'. The correct analysis of these locutions presents special difficulties that I shall not go into, but in any case they indicate a command over a line of action and hence can find employment within practical contexts. The assertion 'I know how to do such and such' offers strong (though not always adequate) backing for the prescription 'Let me do such and such'. The expression 'seeing how' means much the same thing as 'knowing how', but 'seeing how' indicates either that the prescription is backed by visual grounds, or, more often, the expression announces a discovery of a way of carrying out a line of action.

16. THE VALUE OF VALUE JUDGMENTS

In Chapter V, I argued that warrant terms provide much of the diction for reasoned discourse; I shall now say that evaluative terms provide much of the diction for reasoned *practical* discourse. Following the pattern of Chapter V, I shall say that strong evaluative statements can be *assurance* giving, while relatively strong evaluations can give *guarded assurance*, and relatively weak evaluations can have a *discounting* quality. The reader can easily supply his own examples of value judgments functioning in each of these ways.

Value judgments will find employment in any situation where a remark about the status of the backing on behalf of some prescription is apposite. Obviously then, they will find employment in contexts in which an immediate choice is being contemplated. It is to such contexts that I have usually turned for my examples, and there is some justification for considering them primary. But value judgments also bear upon potential choices as well; if I am told that a prescription is warranted on certain grounds, then I have a piece of information that will become useful whenever the line of conduct presents itself in a context where the indicated grounds are relevant.

Justifying our past conduct, together with praising and blaming, provide the main employment for past tense evaluative statements. Consider the business of justifying something we have done: here we are not trying to prove that we did something, we are trying to show that what we did was not wrong. In the language of warrant statement analysis, justifying an action is trying to show that a prescription prohibiting an act (what Kant would call the maxim of the act) was (or is) not warranted.

Finally, there are all sorts of derivative uses of value judgments. At times, a value judgment will be used simply as a descriptive statement. This can occur when the requisite grounds are relatively well defined and well known. The claim that a car is in excellent condition gives a good deal of more or less precise information about the car—but only to a person with a knowledge of the standard criteria for evaluating a car. Evaluative terms are also used expressively, and here, let me suggest, the presentation of the grounds would also be filled with expressive language. We use evaluative terms emotively in just those areas where we argue emotively.

I could go on in this fashion, but it would largely be a matter of paraphrasing Nowell-Smith, Toulmin, and Hare, who have all written upon the varied jobs performed by evaluative statements. I shall, then, drop this subject and turn to the bearing this approach to evaluative statements has upon certain theoretical problems, in particular, the relationship between facts and values.

VIII

FACTS AND VALUES

IN Chapter VII I have tried to show how the warrant statement approach will allow us to characterize evaluative discourse and thereby distinguish it from non-evaluative discourse. In this closing chapter I shall attempt to explain how evaluative and non-evaluative discourse are interconnected, and, to put the cards on the table at once, I wish to recommend a form of ethical naturalism. I shall not present a specific naturalistic theory, instead, I shall content myself with securing the foundations of ethical naturalism against certain attacks that are still popular. I am afraid that much of this will appear naïve in comparison with the subtlety of the arguments that have been used against ethical naturalism, for I shall content myself with some very modest work at the foundations of this subject.

2. FACTS AND VALUES, THE PROBLEM

Traditionally philosophers have worried about the connection between facts and values, asking, for example, about the *place of value in a world of facts*. At least part of the trouble has been generated by giving the terms 'value' and 'fact' a substantival interpretation, but troubles still remain even if we are emancipated in this respect. The problem was formulated by David Hume in a famous passage:

> I cannot forbear adding to these reasonings an observation which may perhaps be found of some importance. In every system

of morality which I have hitherto met with I have always remarked that the author proceeds for some time in the ordinary way of reasoning, and established the being of God, or makes observations concerning human affairs; when of a sudden I am surprised to find, that instead of the usual copulations of propositions *is* and *is not*, I meet with no proposition that is not connected with an *ought*, or an *ought not*. This change is imperceptible; but is, however, of the last consequence. For as this *ought* or *ought not* express some new relation of affirmation, it is necessary that it should be observed and explained; and at the same time that a reason should be given for what seems altogether inconceivable, how this new relation can be a deduction from others that are entirely different from it.[1]

In the context of Hume's *Treatise*, it is not at all clear what we are to make of this passage, for in the development of his own ethical theory he at least seems to make the very transition that is here called into question. But setting aside the problems of interpreting Hume, we may still note that many philosophers have claimed that there is a logical gap between factual claims and evaluative claims, and thus any inference from one to another must be fallacious. Virtually every attack upon ethical naturalism has depended upon pointing to this logical gap with respect to at least some evaluative terms. One strategy for dealing with this issue is to declare that the distinction between evaluative and factual judgments is itself problematic, but this is not a line that is open on the warrant statement approach, for I have argued that evaluative statements can be distinguished from other statements in virtue of a distinctive kind of warrant schema. I shall not here examine the attacks upon the distinctions between facts and values and between descriptive and evaluative statements. Instead I shall try to show how ethical naturalism can be developed when this distinction is accepted as having a *prima facie* plausibility.

Schematically, the problematic character of the inference may be represented as follows:

$$p_1$$
$$p_2$$
.   A set of premises using no
.   evaluative terms.
.

$$\frac{p_n}{\therefore \ E}$$ An evaluative conclusion.

[1] David Hume, *Treatise of Human Nature*, Selby-Bigge edition, pp. 469–70.

Once we consent to deal with the problem in this way, there seems to be no way of certifying the inference, for we seem to be left with two unhappy alternatives: (1) it could be argued that all such inferences depend upon a further suppressed premiss which does employ an evaluative term; or (2) it could be argued that the evaluative conclusion introduces no concepts absent in the premisses.

The first line of argument would run as follows. In every inference from facts to values, there can be found a suppressed premiss that relates facts to values. The premiss would have the following form:

> If a thing has the factual predicate *F*, then it has the evaluative predicate *E*.

With this suppressed premiss included, the fallacious character of the argument disappears, but the problem has not been solved, only pushed back a step where it reasserts itself as strongly as before. If the suppressed premiss asserts only a contingent relationship between the predicate *F* and the predicate *E*, the logical gap remains open. We can imagine a world where everything coloured blue also smells rancid, but this correlation would show no logical connection between colours and smells. If, on the other hand, it is claimed that the hypothetical statement asserts a necessary connection, we then ask how this can be, since the consequent non-vacuously contains a predicate not present in the antecedent.

The second line will not do either, at least on the warrant statement approach. I have argued that evaluative statements do have a distinctive character, and thus they cannot be entailed by a set of premisses that lack this character.

This reasoning seems to have disastrous results, for it not only forces us to say that we cannot *deduce* an evaluative conclusion from purely factual premisses; if pressed relentlessly, it would yield the result that facts simply have nothing to do with values. It might turn out that things that possess value also always have certain factual properties, but we demand a connection closer than this, for in order to reflect normal evaluative reasoning we want to be able to say that things are good *because* they possess certain factual properties. It is just this connection that seems impossible to make out.

Facts and Values

3. A PARALLEL PROBLEM

This problem has the two marks of a philosophic puzzle: the results are preposterous, but the reasoning involved seems flawless. Faced with such a puzzle, it often helps to find a parallel case that can shed light upon the structure of the problem. The transition from *is* to *must* presents such a parallel case.

This shift is often found at the completion of a sustained inquiry. The closing paragraphs of a detective story often exhibit this pattern; the detective has completed his investigation, and to the astonishment of the local constable, declares that the case is solved. His argument runs as follows:

p_1
p_2 A set of evidential statements arranged in the form
p_3 of an argument. These assertions do not contain
.   the term 'must' or any other alethic terms.

.

p_n
____

∴ M A conclusion stating that a particular person *must* be the murderer.

Again we assume that Hume would be surprised to find the usual connectives *is* and *is not* replaced by the new connective *must* in the conclusion; for how can a relationship appear in the conclusion when it is absent in the premises? Once more, if we accept the framework of the argument, there will be no way of avoiding the Humean scepticism, and we will be driven to say that matters of fact have nothing to do with assertions that something must be the case.

But a way out of this difficulty can be found if we reflect upon the warrant character of many statements that contain the word 'must'. Suppose, in the first place, that it is possible to construct a sound argument of the following form:

p_1
p_2 A set of premises containing no alethic
.   modal terms.

.

p_n
____

∴ Herbert Crenshaw is the murderer.

If we are able to produce such an argument, then we can truthfully say that there are adequate grounds available on behalf of the assertion that Herbert Crenshaw is the murderer, but on the warrant statement approach, this is equivalent to saying that Herbert Crenshaw must be the murderer. We have thus made a transition from the *is* to the *must*.

Of course, the two statements, 'Herbert Crenshaw *is* the murderer', and 'Herbert Crenshaw *must be* the murderer', stand in different relationships to the premisses p_1 to p_n. The first statement is derived *from* the premisses, while the second statement is an assertion *about* the relationship between a set of premisses and a conclusion. They are remarks, then, of a different logical order. Yet the crucial point is this: producing a sound argument for the first statement is all that is needed to establish the truth of the second, thus, in admittedly different senses, both statements can be said to *follow from* the set of premisses.

4. A PARALLEL SOLUTION

The discussion of inferences from *is* to *must* suggests an answer to the problem concerning the supposed logical gap between non-evaluative premisses and an evaluative conclusion. Since this is a complicated business, let me proceed by stages. First, consider an argument of the following form:

$$p_1$$
$$p_2$$
.   A set of non-evaluative premisses.

.

$$p_n$$

∴ Imp.   A conclusion in the imperative.

If an argument of this form is sound, then we can truthfully say that there are adequate grounds available on behalf of the pre-scription 'Imp.', and this, under the warrant statement analysis of value judgments is equivalent to a value judgment. The value judgment is not derived directly from the set of non-evaluative premisses, but—like the *must* statement in the previous section—it is true in virtue of the existence of such a set of premisses. Thus we have a right to assert a value judgment on the basis of a set of non-evaluative statements even though the value judgment is not entailed by these non-evaluative statements.

The next step in this argument is to show that it is possible to construct a sound argument on behalf of an imperative without employing an evaluation in the premises. We can show this provided that we recognize an important principle: *it is impossible to deduce a prescriptive conclusion from wholly non-prescriptive premises.* It is for this reason—not because of some ontological gap—that a value judgment cannot be derived from wholly factual premises. Factual judgments usually lack the prescriptive force latent in every value judgment. The following argument obeys this principle and is, it seems to me, an example of a valid argument with a prescriptive conclusion:

(1) A Ford or a Cadillac are the only options. (Options)
(2) From the options, buy the item that costs (Criterion)
     the least!
(3) A Ford costs less than a Cadillac. (Relevant fact)

∴ Buy a Ford rather than a Cadillac.

In a context where we would accept the factual premisses (1) and (3) and also accept (2), the prescriptive premiss, we could then say that the argument is not only valid, but sound as well. Furthermore, with this argument as a backing, we could say that there are adequate grounds on behalf of the prescription, 'Buy a Ford rather than a Cadillac!' and this, under the warrant statement approach, is equivalent to saying that the Ford is a better buy than the Cadillac. Thus the transition has been made from non-evaluative premisses to an evaluative conclusion.

But I am afraid that the above argument may seem unconvincing, and the reason for this is not some technical flaw in the reasoning, but rather, the great unlikelihood that a person would accept so simple a criterion of selection as that presented in the second premiss. Yet nobody would have challenged the following conclusion: if you are interested solely in price, then a Ford is a better buy than a Cadillac, and this is all that I need in order to establish my conclusion. Now if I ask, for the sake of argument, that the second premiss be accepted, i.e. that price be made the sole criterion of selection, then the non-hypothetical conclusion, 'A Ford is a better buy than a Cadillac' is established.

Let me summarize this discussion: it is possible to make a transition from facts to values if the facts *in conjunction with at least one further prescriptive premiss* constitute a sound argument on behalf of a prescriptive conclusion. In such a case we can say that there are adequate grounds available on behalf of a given prescription, and this, on the warrant statement analysis of evaluative statements, is equivalent to making a value judgment. Thus, the *is* can imply the *ought*, but only enthymematically and indirectly.

5. THE ULTIMATE JUSTIFICATION OF PRESCRIPTIONS

On the approach here outlined, every question of value ultimately rests upon the claim that some prescription is *materially* justified, and this brings us to the rock bottom question: how does one materially justify telling someone (perhaps oneself) to do a certain thing? This is a theoretical question, for in everyday affairs we get along quite well by citing one prescriptive utterance as backing for another—we back up our imperatives by value judgments, and our value judgments by other value judgments—but this procedure does not help us find the basis for accepting any prescriptions as such.

I think that Kant has been one of the few philosophers to recognize the logical character of the basic question of ethics; he saw that the fundamental question of ethics concerned the grounds of a categorical imperative. His own solution, which I shall not discuss in detail, was to seek the ground of an imperative in its *a priori* character; thus, it seems to me, he confused logical necessity with moral necessity. The confusion is natural enough because the German language permits many of the same interchanges of warrant terms that I have pointed to in the English language.

In contrast with Kant's *a priori* approach I would like to side with the tradition that grounds values in human nature,[1] and in particular in the teleological or purposive side of human nature. Let me offer the following thesis as a speculative hypothesis: *if a person desires to do a certain thing, this will constitute* prima facie[2] *adequate grounds on behalf of an imperative that prescribes doing this very thing.* Or to translate this out of warrant statement language into common parlance: *if a person desires a thing, he will consider that thing*

---

[1] In taking sides, I cross the line from metaethics to ethics.

[2] Here I use the phrase '*prima facie* grounds' in the legal sense of grounds sufficient to raise a presumption of fact, unless rebutted.

a prima facie *good*. Human desires, I am suggesting, bridge the gap between facts and values by supplying the *prima facie* grounds for the acceptability of a prescription.

I make no claim for the originality of this speculative thesis. Hobbes, for example, seemed to be saying much the same thing when he declared that whatever a man desires he takes for his own part to be good, and in essence, Ralph Barton Perry offers just this account of the ground of value in the fifth chapter of his *General Theory of Value*:

> This, then, we take to be the original source and constant feature of all value. That which is an object of interest is *eo ipso* invested with value. Any object, whatever it be, acquires value when any interest, whatever it be, is taken in it; . . .[1]

Here Perry is trying to exhibit the generic character of value, and he is not trying to define any particular species of it. Thus, it is beside the point to attack Perry by pointing out that we often desire things that we realize are not valuable. Perry takes great pains to indicate that the value bestowed by one interest can be overridden by the disvalue bestowed by a negative interest. Interest bestows a *prima facie* good on an object; it is sufficient unless rebutted by some other interest.

I am thus recommending a variation of naturalism in the study of human values, a naturalism that would ground the whole structure of values—including moral values, aesthetic values, political values, etc.—upon the desires of individual human beings. But I do not propose to make a substantive contribution to the development of such a theory; instead, I shall simply show that the warrant statement approach will allow for the development of a naturalism free from the charges levelled against it in Chapter VI.

6. THE LOGICAL BASIS OF A NATURALISTIC VALUE THEORY

To begin with, it must be conceded that ethical naturalists often present their theories in a way that makes them subject to Moore's criticism. Perry, for example, declares:

> The fundamental problem of theory of value is to define the *concept* of value.[2]

[1] Ralph Barton Perry, *General Theory of Value* (New York, 1926), p. 116.
[2] Ibid., p. 16.

This in itself does not show that Perry wishes to present a semantical thesis, for the phrase 'define the *concept* of value' is sufficiently ambiguous to cover a number of enterprises. But on one occasion he chooses to couch his theory in the explicit form of a linguistic thesis:

'X is valuable' = 'Interest is taken in X'.[1]

If this is not a claim for synonymy, it is hard to understand what interpretation to put on the quotation marks and the identity sign.

And if Perry is arguing that the statement 'X is valuable' is synonymous with the statement 'Interest is taken in X', then we must say that he is plainly mistaken; and not only a little bit wrong, but wrong in principle. I am not here being dogmatic, for I can cite the entire line of argument of Chapters V and VI in support for the claim that value judgments cannot be treated as a kind of direct factual judgment. Furthermore, the use of the above synonymy claim has disastrous results for Perry's theory; it converts the claim that an object acquires value when interest is taken in it into a bare tautology. It is hard to believe that Perry has written a seven-hundred-page work ranging over such fields as biology, psychology, and sociology under the misapprehension that these empirical fields will have a bearing upon the truth of an analytic judgment.

An idea introduced in the preceding section provides a way of making sense out of (and vindicating) Perry's theoretical endeavours. Without explicitly realizing it, Perry, along with other ethical naturalists, was searching for the ultimate grounds for the acceptance of a prescription. As such, his theory can be properly stated in the following way:

X is generically valuable if, and only if, interest is taken in X.

Notice that this is not a semantical thesis at all, it is a synthetic claim about what things are generically valuable. Thus it is not subject to the criticism that Moore pressed against naturalism, namely, the charge of reducing value judgments to factual judgments. Moore would consider the above schema an example of defining *the* good, and as we have noted he had no systematic objections to this kind of definition.[2]

[1] Ralph Barton Perry, p. 116.
[2] All things considered, it would probably be preferable not to call such assertions definitions at all.

A general theory of value, then, will have the following form:

X is generically valuable if, and only if, X is ϕ.

On a naturalistic approach, 'ϕ' would be some empirical property or system of empirical properties, but the schema provides an equally good outline for a non-naturalistic value theory; for example, 'X is good if, and only if, X participates in the divine perfection of God'. Warrant statement analysis is, and ought to be, neutral with respect to the way in which 'ϕ' is filled in. Hence it is neutral with respect to the specific content of any given value theory.

Since the formula 'X is generically valuable if, and only if, X is ϕ' avoids the standard criticisms of naturalism, it seems odd that philosophers have not adopted it but instead have persistently couched their theories in just the form that makes them subject to Moore's criticisms. This, I suggest, is the result of a failure to understand the warrant character of value judgments. If the assumption is made that goodness is a material property, then the schema 'X is good if, and only if, X is ϕ' seems to assert too loose a relationship between goodness and this other property ϕ; it merely asserts a constant conjunction between goodness and ϕ and tells us nothing directly about goodness itself. Under the warrant statement approach this two-property image disappears, and we see that the function of a general theory of value is to discover the generic grounds for following one line of conduct rather than another.

Thus the warrant statement approach provides a *tertium quid* between intuitionism and an old-fashioned naturalism. From intuitionism we can accept the doctrine that evaluations cannot be treated as simple assertions of fact, but we need not follow intuitionism into the doctrine of non-natural properties or some similar mystery. From naturalism we can accept the notion that values are grounded in human nature, in particular, in the teleological character of human nature, but we can do this without committing the fallacy of reductionism.

Finally, the warrant statement approach provides a way of distinguishing between the various evaluative sciences without introducing a system of peculiar entities. There will be as many kinds of value as there are kinds of reasons that can be brought forward on behalf of a prescription. Ethics, then, is not a search after an elusive entity called ethical value, nor is aesthetics a matter of squinting at a painting in order to find its beauty. In each case, the proper object of study is the character of the grounds that gives the species of value its distinctive quality. The study of the grounds that warrant a prescription lacks the profundity (and hence the attraction) of the traditional ontological approach, but unlike the latter approach, it is not based on a mistake, and hence may bear fruit.

Before closing this topic, let me suggest one further reason why the naturalistic approach to ethics has been largely unsuccessful. With but few exceptions naturalists have been insensitive to the richness and subtlety of evaluative discourse and for this reason have failed to recognize that there is a vast distance between their theoretical notion of a generic value and the full specification of the higher-order evaluative notions. To cite but one, rather crude example, deontic statements are sometimes rendered as conditional predictions:

'John morally ought to do x' $=$ 'If John does not do x, then a moral sanction will be applied to him.'

We can see that this analysis is wrong straight off since a warrant statement is equated with a statement that is not a warrant statement. But even beyond this, unless the word 'sanction' does yeoman service, the analysis will be entirely too simple-minded. The notions of a moral ought and a moral sanction are high-order concepts that can be understood only by seeing their place within a whole system of moral concepts. Unless the naturalist in ethics can learn to find his way about within the network of evaluative notions, his whole programme will be rejected on the basis of its crudity alone.

To sum up, I think that the naturalistic programme in ethics has fallen upon evil days for two reasons, first, because of a tendency to make a mistake in the analysis of evaluative discourse, and secondly, through a failure to take the proper measure of the difficulty of the programme they are undertaking. In this chapter I have tried only to remedy the first defect by showing how such a theory can *get started*; if you like, I have been pottering around in the basement of the naturalistic approach to ethics.

Facts and Values

7. A CLOSING DISCLAIMER

So far we have been going firmly ahead, feeling the firm ground of prejudice glide away beneath our feet which is always rather exhilarating, but what next? You will be waiting for the bit when we bog down, the bit where we take it all back . . .[1]

Throughout this work I have been using the notions of grounds, reasons, and evidence as if they were unproblematic. Of course, they are not. Consider as a case in point the rich variety of factors that enter into, say, a moral assessment: intentions, motives, consequences, special relationships, prior commitments, established rules, states of character, states of knowledge, psychological and physical possibility, etc., can all be cited in reasons for or against a prescription, and thereby take on the status of grounds. Thus, for a complete analysis of moral assessments, it would be necessary to sort out these different kinds of reasons and then specify in detail how each kind bears upon a prescription. This I have not done, nor am I able to do it. Furthermore, the same difficulties will arise with respect to any of the warrant schemata that I have presented. In every case the grounds invoked take a variety of forms and operate as grounds in a variety of ways. Warrant statement analysis demands for its completeness a taxonomy of reasons.

By restricting my attention to just a few properties of warrant statements and by using artificially simple examples, I have been able to avoid bogging down. Thus, if I have given the impression that some of the major problems of philosophy have been solved once and for all, I must now take it back. I have merely presented programmes for future study and left most of the difficult work undone.

[1] J. L. Austin, *Philosophical Papers*, Clarendon Press (Oxford, 1961), p. 228.

INDEX

Index

187